# Acculturative Stress and Change in Nigerian Society

# Acculturative Stress and Change in Nigerian Society

Ezekiel Ette

LEXINGTON BOOKS
*Lanham • Boulder • New York • London*

Published by Lexington Books
An imprint of The Rowman & Littlefield Publishing Group, Inc.
4501 Forbes Boulevard, Suite 200, Lanham, Maryland 20706
www.rowman.com

6 Tinworth Street, London SE11 5AL, United Kingdom

Copyright © 2020 The Rowman & Littlefield Publishing Group, Inc.

*All rights reserved.* No part of this book may be reproduced in any form or by any electronic or mechanical means, including information storage and retrieval systems, without written permission from the publisher, except by a reviewer who may quote passages in a review.

British Library Cataloguing in Publication Information Available

**Library of Congress Cataloging-in-Publication Data**

Library of Congress Control Number:2019950454
ISBN 978-1-4985-7861-5 (cloth)
ISBN 978-1-4985-7862-2 (electronic)

For Bea Arnie and William and Elaine Berry,
who saw beyond skin color

# Contents

| | | |
|---|---|---|
| 1 | Identity, Culture, and History | 1 |
| 2 | Annang Social and Political Organization before Colonialism | 17 |
| 3 | British Colonialism | 31 |
| 4 | The Invasion of Annangland | 43 |
| 5 | Western Education and the New Class | 55 |
| 6 | Confronting Change | 67 |
| 7 | Power and Politics as Philanthropy | 85 |
| 8 | Group Relationships and Dynamics | 95 |
| 9 | The Identity Question | 113 |
| 10 | Postindependence and Civil War | 125 |
| 11 | The Future | 135 |
| References | | 149 |
| Index | | 157 |
| About the Author | | 159 |

## Chapter One

# Identity, Culture, and History

The idea of nation-states, where groups were able to establish political territories based on ethnicity, was abolished by European colonialism in Africa (Ette, 2010). Ironically, however, colonialism in Africa occurred at a period in world history that is considered the apex of the nation-state movement (Young, 1985). The Europeans formed states defined along ethnic lines at home and pushed ethnic nationalism while denying the same arrangements to Africans who were forced together based on the European need for territories abroad. Ethnic groups in Africa were forced together without regard to historical antecedents and opinion in the new political arrangements. Countries were created and new territories became nations without the consent of the citizens. The Africans found themselves together under alien names and in new countries. Political realities under such conditions, especially in Sub-Saharan Africa in the words of Mbembe (2001), became "a number of socially produced and objectified practices" (p. 6). Beginning in 1957 with Ghanaian independence, countries in Sub-Saharan Africa later shook the yoke of colonialism and became politically independent. With independence, the quilting of ethnicities into political units became established and calcified without, however, disappearing. Artificial ethnic boundaries created by the colonialists remained and the indigenous politicians exploited this new arrangement. Furthermore, political issues became ethnicized and policy decisions continue to be made through the prism of ethnicity rather than on merits or economic sense. The political elites in the postcolonial states in Africa push ethnic issues and those with the numerical strength tilt toward domination and homogenization, thereby making ethnic minorities to see themselves as oppressed with no stake in national policies. Currently, the Euro-American ideal of the nation-state in Africa becomes a dream as political leaders care more about tribal geographical issues than the national ones.

Ironically, as globalization diminishes space and time and makes the world smaller, the ancient issues of ethnicity, rather than being banished to the dust bins of history, continue to play a dominant role in African politics. Ethnicity and politics, specifically the rights of the minorities within larger political units, have been acknowledged as a focus of attention since the middle of the last century. The UN declaration of the rights of self-determination among people, calling for sensitivity on the rights of minority populations, lends credence to this fact and highlights the importance of this issue. Despite efforts at addressing the issues of diversity and tolerance at the global level, ethnic violence continues to plague the world. As Travis (2013) reminded us, there had not been many hostilities in the last century whose origin did not include interethnic disagreements. This is especially true in Africa, which has seen numerous conflicts with origins in ethnicity. Wars and killings in Liberia, Nigeria, the Congo, and Rwanda are recent examples.

The literature on ethnicity and diversity has long recognized the importance of culture in human behavior and has stressed culturally competent approaches in dealing with individuals from other cultures (Bennet, 2017; Betancourt and López, 1993). However, much still remains to be done in the area of ethnic conflict avoidance and resolution. For now, the basic approach has been a call for training in diversity. As events have shown in the last few decades, conflicts have arisen along ethnic lines in different parts of the world as a result of direct appeals to racism or politicians taking advantage of ethnic differences to pursue selfish political agenda by pushing policies that favor one's ethnic group over the others (Healy, 2001). Thus, conflicts have arisen in Europe, Asia, South America, and Africa. Though Mbembe (2001) attributes most of these interethnic conflicts in Africa to the dismantling of external structures imposed by colonialism, mention must also be made of the influence of globalization, postmodernism, and the movements of individuals across boundaries. Additionally, public policies are seen primarily through the lens of ethnicity as already mentioned, such that what does or does not make sense depends on what group is affected and who is affected. In Nigeria, for example, the dismantling of the colonial policing structures by the Aguiyi Ironsi administration in 1966 led to the police force operating on a unitary system in a multiethnic society to this day. The head of state in this new arrangement appoints the inspector general of police and then later is answerable only to that appointing authority. Governors at the state level have little or no control over the police in their various states. The states do not have prisons and cannot operate any by law. The state structure introduced by General Gowon in 1967 dismantled the regional federating system imposed by the colonialist. In the new state structure, ethnicity rather than geography or agriculture becomes the basis of state creation. Thus, those with political power have more states and therefore allocation from the federal treasury and the minority populations are often neglected no matter their economic contribution to the national wealth. This practice inherently leads to neglect of communities and groups in the Nigerian Niger delta.

In an ironic reversal, while the nation-state in Europe is diminishing because of globalization, the African political elites are trying to create homogenous enclaves within their own countries in an attempt to establish majority-minority groups. The goal is to introduce dominance and in the process make citizens from other regions strangers in their own countries. Nigeria has created "states" using this formula and the minorities in such states must choose between adopting the majority language and culture or face social exclusion. Lacking legitimacy, the postcolony, as Mbembe (2001) called it, crumbles with demands for freedom and self-determination by states forced together and resulted in the resurrection of ancient animosities. Mehta (1997) stated that this animosity can follow a three-stage process of ethnic superiority, ethnic cleansing, and finally genocide. Thus, we witnessed the violence against Muslims by Serbs in Bosnia, Hutus against Tutsis in Rwanda, and Albanians and Serbs in Kosovo as recent examples. In Burundi and Rwanda, two countries with Hutu majorities and Tutsi minorities, the cycle of massacres has appeared and reappeared from 1959, 1963, 1872, 1988, 1993, and1994 (*The Economist*, 2016).

In order to illustrate our point well and contextualize the idea, this book discusses the effect of colonialism in Africa and the resulting acculturative stress using the Annang of southeast Nigeria as a case example. I seek to argue that in the aftermath of European domination and colonial rule, what the Africans are struggling with and the relationships between groups in Africa can be traced to the events in the colonial history as well as events in the postcolonial struggle for domination by the elites. The book thus traces the history of the Annang struggle for ethnic identity and recognition in postcolonial Nigeria from precolonial times to the post–civil war period. It further argues that colonialism destroyed the Annang identity but the struggle for power following colonialism has also raised other problems with serious consequences. What happened to the Annang represents an example that was repeated all over Africa. As the discussion will show, what is happening among the Annang is symptomatic of the African struggle.

This book is beyond the usual discussion of the effects of colonialism in the continent that often sees the modern state as a monolithic whole. It is presented as a real-life example of the effects of colonialism and power relationships and therefore a window through which to see the African problems in modern times. The Annang world changed as a result of colonialism, but relationships and power within the modern Nigerian state have also affected the meaning of self, ethnicity, and nationality. Because of colonialism, what was real and unreal became blurred to the Annang and their values and ultimately their identity were called into question. As the discussion will show, what defined wealth, personhood, and even life itself had to be done using an alien system and new values. Who the Annang individual was had to be defined and redefined using values brought by the Europeans. New identities were imposed on them by their new conquerors. Thus, the Annang had to look for new survival techniques like a drowning person must clutch on a straw. New political alliances were created as survival tools. When colonialism ended, the elites who took power from the colonialists maintained colonial boundaries, redesigned new ones, and continued the creation of new identities for their own benefit. These events and alliances, as the discussion will demonstrate, have become an important factor in the Annang identity. Among the Annang group as elsewhere in Africa, ethnicity is more than simply a social recognition of cultural and historical relatedness; it carries enormous political implications (Ekanem, 2002).

## IMPORTANCE OF ETHNICITY

We shall examine three views of this issue. We will begin with Moynihan (1993), Ake (2002), and later the postmodernist view. The first maintains that particular attention should be paid to ethnicity, the second sees it as transitory and as a child of circumstance, while the last recommends that it is a crucial part of the individual's identity.

Writing about his Jewish identity, Sigmund Freud stated that his sense of identity resulted from "many obscure emotional forces which were the more powerful the less they could be expressed in words" (quoted in Moynihan, 1993). Thus, one's identity draws from the identity of the community. There is, therefore, according to Erikson (1958), a deep and powerful commonality known only to members of the group. In a sense, this deep understanding has a spiritual orientation for it answers the salient spiritual question of "who am I?" Thus, the individual is not only somebody's brother, sister, husband, wife, uncle, or aunt but is also a member of a particular ethnic group whose values and culture are derived from those of the community (Ette, 2001). As Isaac (1975) noted, "the function of basic group identity has to do most crucially with two key ingredients in every individual's personality and life experience: his sense of belongingness and the quality of his self-esteem" (p. 42). Thus, I am defined and known as coming from one locality or community and not another. I speak one language and use its symbols as a way of making sense of the world. I am associated with one ethnic group and not all the others. The history of my people is, therefore, mine for it tells me and those who know me where I come from, how my forebears survived, and what they did to survive. I become part of who I am today because of what was transmitted to me through their experience and what became their culture determines how I see the world and how I interact with that world. In sum, my survival depends on how I learn the lessons transmitted to me. Yet my struggle in the socialization process is at the same time both mine and that of the group. Through a shared experience and ability to interpret the world together, I feel a sense of belongingness and become a part of a group. I see myself through values shared by the group and therefore derive my self-worth as an individual from the group. The danger lies in seeing my group as the center of the universe and so I must also realize that others have group identities too and therefore must negotiate without actually surrendering my identity and history.

Despite the importance of ethnicity as a form of group identity, the intellectual class in the West has tended to regard it as primitive and transitory (Moynihan, 1993). Thus, the word "ethnic" has come to assume a connotation of the primitive as opposed to "civilized." In the United States, a society built mostly by immigrants, for example, the intellectual class believes that individuals around the world brought to the country through the American immigration process would in time shed their ethnicity and thus there would be *publius unum* or from many one. The immigrants, having shed old primitive bearings and trajectories, would make themselves *ethnic less* and become ingredients for the melting pot (Moynihan, 1993). This idea of the melting pot is beyond a merely intellectual exercise as events have shown in the United States. Failure to conform to social mores leads to social exclusion, which Gore (1995) defined as the loss of social solidarity and rupture of social relationship by a part of the population that no longer participates in significant opportunities available in the society. Therefore the threat of social exclusion forces conformity and adoption of new identities. There is, for example, a direct relationship between the ability to speak English and the ability to gain employment in the United States. How did the West get it so wrong? How did they fail to note the importance of ethnicity, especially among Africans?

To answer this question, we must turn to history and specifically the history of Western sociological thought. Augustus Comte, regarded as a pioneer in the field of sociology, had postulated in the nineteenth century that cultures pass through successive stages of theological thought, metaphysical thought, and positivist thought (Bourdeau, 2015). This Comtean theory maintained that cultures of the world could be arranged in a continuum from the primitive to the most civilized. Applying this logic, African cultures were seen as being from primitive societies with the world seen from theological lenses, and the Europeans were seen as the advanced and civilized cultures through the prism of positivism. Comte maintained that the European culture could be studied best by looking at the primitive ones that serve as a window to the past. Because all human cultures began at the same time, he theorized that the "primitive" ones encountered a "crisis" that halted its progress toward civilization and therefore came to a standstill. The higher cultures continued to advance and reached civilization while the others became arrested and stagnated (Jones, 1998; Harris, 2001). Thus, positivism, with a combination of ethnocentric and evolutionary theories, lay the foundation whereby ethnicity and its claims were seen as primitive. Today, the word "tribe" continues this understanding. The word is used exclusively for Africans and Native Americans and carries a connotation of primitiveness and backwardness. It can be argued that, like Comte, we can now place the cultures of the world in a continuum with the tribe at one end and names of countries with claims to "civilization" on the other. While the Africans and other indigenous cultures are referred to as "tribes," others are moved up a notch and seen as "ethnic," with the Western countries claiming the higher status as nationals of their respective states at the end of the chain. And so we can speak about the American, French, English, and German culture as superior to the uncivilized and tribal cultures that are not worthy of rigorous academic study except as a window to the past; we can look at the ethnic groups within the "tribal" cultures as dismissible.

The second perspective holds that ethnicity is transitory. Ake (1992) reminded us that ethnicity "is not a fossilized determination" but rather is brought about by historical forces. What is regarded as ethnicity, the understanding continues, is transitory because what we know as ethnicity "begins, becomes and passes away" (Ake, 1992, p. 1). Who is Annang, Efik, Ibibio, Igbo, Hutu, or Tutsi in this understanding depends on the time and facts of history. Some historical forces might have been at work that eventually established characteristics of exclusion, inclusion, and boundaries. Those so defined accept their commonality, but because such action and agreement is carried on by living beings, such an agreed-upon identity is subject to the principle of impermanence, which does not allow the living to be static. Thus, ethnicity like other things about life changes, grows weak, and dies. Ethnicity, according to this understanding, therefore, is subject to the forces of history. Groups migrate and adopt new cultural practices because culture is a buffer to environmental conditions. Those who live in desert areas with sandstorms, for example, need something to cover their eyes in the event of a sandstorm. Therefore the need for survival requires that individuals take along something to cover the eyes and that eventually becomes the head covering seen among those who live in the Sahara regions of the world. Those who live in cold climates require warm clothing to stay warm in the winter, and therefore suits and ties become necessities. Furthermore, individuals eat what grows in their environment and how they are prepared depends on what is available. Thus, cultural cuisine follows the same trajectory. Given these facts, migration and changes in environmental conditions can and do dictate cultural practices, language, and subsequently identity. This may account for similarities in cultures and relatedness in languages. Reverend Hope Masterson Waddell, the Scottish missionary who translated the Christian Bible into the Efik language in the nineteenth century, was surprised to discover lots of similarities in sound and sense between the language and biblical Hebrew (Waddell, 1863).

The third and final view of ethnicity relates to the postmodernist view. Postmodernism has come to alter our understanding of human cultures and our understanding of ethnicity, so holds another school of thought (Lukacs, 2003). The term itself, "postmodernism," assumes that something has happened after modernism. Reese (1980) opined that it is common for individuals to assume that anyone who takes the norm of modern life and thought could be said to be operating within modernism, yet modernism emanated from the religious thoughts of the German religious critical movement. It was used for those who applied the historical critical method for interpreting the scripture and church dogma made popular by German theologians such as Adolf Harnack. The stress of this religious movement tended to be on the experiential and social relevance of the Gospel rather than the creedal and dogmatic aspects (Reese, 1980). Though the Catholic Church condemned modernism as evidenced by the encyclical of Pope Pius X in 1907, the movement spread. In literature, the movement was concerned with how to correctly portray reality and truth in writing (Kidder and Oppenheim, 2005). Though the movement questioned the concept of objective reality, it nevertheless maintained that we can know through study, analysis, and experimentation. Science could be called into the service of humans in a fragmented world. Most scholars maintained that 1940 ended the period of modernism.

Postmodernism, then, can be said to be a reaction to the thinking of the modernists, and its beginning is located at the end of World War II. The carnage of the war brought by the brutality of humans exposed the hypocrisy of those who espoused learning and study and brought into question the definition of civilization. Those who were under the yoke of colonialism in Africa and elsewhere found themselves in trenches in Europe fighting alongside their colonial masters who had no higher moral standing than those they once referred to as savages. Postmodernism, therefore, rather than be seen as a movement should be seen as a reaction to modernism. With its beginnings after World War II, it was galvanized and sped up by the awareness of the effects of unbridled scientific destruction of the war years. Other events that manifested and help its spread included the civil rights movement, the sexual revolution of the 1960s, and the reactions to the silence of the religious class to the oppression and poverty of the underclass in Europe and the United States. The antiwar movements of the 1970s and the ideologies that argued for conflict and ignored public opinion also helped to change the thinking of the young and progressive class. Postmodernism is characterized by the following ideas according to Lukacs (2003).

1. The end of European dominance in world affairs. Following World War II, the influence of European powers subsided and the United States began playing an increasing role in the postwar period. The creation of the United Nations and the opening up of that organization to newly independent developing countries gave these countries a voice at the world stage. Europe was no longer the center of power on the world stage (Lukacs, 2003). New York found the new countries coming to meetings at the UN and the concept of self-determination entered the lexicon.
2. The place of applied science in the progress of humans was questioned. Writers questioned modern technology and whether it was a force for good or ill. Where the modernists saw study, analysis, and experimentation as avenues and pathway to truth, the postmodernists maintains that human invention does not necessarily lead to human progress. Rather than bring progress, applied science can be a part of human problems and danger as demonstrated in genetic engineering, nuclear bombs, and smart bombs.
3. The American influence led to the belief that representative democracy is the ideal form of government. This allowed for individuals, groups, and countries to work toward spreading democracy around the world and today many aspire toward democracy.
4. Voices that were once neglected became prominent and all stories become important. Kings and queens are no longer the ones making the news and history. Those who were formerly neglected in the modernist's narratives are given their voice. Minority groups such as homosexuals, lesbians, Hispanics, and blacks can now tell their stories alongside the stories of those with power. Every voice is seen as important. Therefore I can proudly say that I am an Annang person and speak about my culture without being seen as uncivilized. I can speak my language and advocate for its preservation without fear. In 2016, for example, this author's group organized the first Annang Festival of Arts and Culture. The idea was to help the young people learn about aspects of their culture threatened by globalization in a week-long event of activities and a symposium.
5. What once gave power to the few is in decline. Among these are the powers of the state, the importance of the city as people move to the suburbs,

privacy, family (the changing definitions of a family), the function of schools and their benefits, and the printed book.

6. Institutions of the past that had enormous influence such as the church are losing their power. Churches are emptying and it does not help when dogmas that once guided the church have been questioned by those within and outside the church. Martin Luther King Jr. questioned the church's relevance in matters such as racism because the church kept quiet and in some cases supported racism. He opposed oral piety where there was racial injustice. Therefore some saw the church as losing its moral authority (King, 1963).

7. Humans are healthier and living longer and infant mortality is in decline. Certain things that provided comfort to the rich in the past are now available to the middle class.

8. Access to information is available such that we are exposed to stories from around the world every day as a result of technology. Communication is improved and the world is more accessible to people no matter where they live. The limitations of time and space that the modernists struggled with seem now to have been conquered through technology for the postmodernist. A new term known as "globalization" is a part of the lexicon, yet globalization is not without its pitfalls as problems that once belonged to the pages of *National Geographic* such as diseases and terrorism become everyday reality.

9. Capital now pursues labor and the idea of national boundaries is becoming increasingly fluid.

10. The recognition that how people act and how they think are products of their history is now a reality. Facts in this regard are neither absolute nor timeless and truth becomes an agreement between two people.

11. The rejection of meta-narratives (grand theories that seek to explain the existence of something). Lyotard (1979) calls for *petit recit* or the simple stories and not grand narratives. It calls for the rethinking of epistemology, progress, science, and the human place in the universe. The old stories of race and gender are rejected and diversity is seen as important. Such grand concepts as civilization and primitivism in which cultures were divided into categories according to the old Comtean typology are discarded in favor of diversity. As the late Senator Patrick Monyihan (1993) reminded us, ethnicity becomes important and rather than stress the melting pot concept where the *publius unum* idea is orchestrated, we gravitate toward multiculturalism or the salad bowl. Difference is celebrated and seen as strength.

12. Technology has philosophical implications and requires the reexamination of prior assumptions.

13. Spirituality and culture become important because old assumptions have been challenged. The need for meaning, rather than being understood and seen through grand stories, requires personal contemplation and relevance in light of the individual experience. Yet no one institution has the answer and individuals become free to make meanings as they see fit. It is in the light of these that we can tell our stories and sing our own song. It is within this understanding that we all can ask the question "Who am I?"

Given this postmodern understanding, ethnicity is neither calcified nor transitory as noted earlier but becomes a way of understanding the other and their history. It offers cultural humility so that ethnocentrism becomes a thing of the past. We are neither civilized nor primitive in the old Comtean understanding but understand the neighbor as being a product of his or her history and society. We now can speak of diversity and truly from many we become one as citizens of the universe. Postmodernism, therefore, as already stated, has provided a heightened awareness to issues of identity and belongingness. We recognize the role of history in how the building blocks of injustice were gathered and we work through such recognition in tearing down oppression and stereotypes. We are not dismissive of difference but rather pay particular attention to the policies and meanings attached to human differences. We become keenly aware of what is naturalized and what is socially constructed.

Given these facts, Africans are still struggling to rise from certain designations that were imposed by past worldviews. Many were brought together under alien names and were told that they needed to change their ways and become "civilized." With a nonarchival culture, their history and struggles for self-actualization in the civilizing process were lost and we found ourselves asking, "Who am I?" Given the importance of ethnicity and the claims and counterclaims of others about our identity, the search for our true selves becomes more than an academic exercise and calls for a search of our true identity. This chapter will look at the history of the Annang group of southeast Nigeria and argues that colonialism and the work of European amateur ethnographers who came to report on what they considered the curiosities of the primitive distorted the Annang history. When the colonialist left, the Nigerian political elites adopted the colonialists' tactics and further distorted our identity.

## ANNANG EARLY HISTORY

The Annangs have lived in what is present-day Nigeria for a long time. In fact, Udo (1983) maintains that they have been there for more than seven thousand years. One reason for the lack of agreement concerning the length of time has been the absence of an archival record (Messenger, 1957). The Annangs live in southeast Nigeria between the Igbos in the west and the Ibibios to the east. Their number is more than one million according to the 1995 Nigerian census. Various writers have described them as Ibibios, but the Annangs have rejected this categorization and insist on being recognized as a separate group (Brink, 1982). European writers and amateur ethnographers with their imperfect knowledge of African geography, history, and language have tended to label and assign names to groups that they knew very little about (Groves, 1936; Perham, 1936). In describing the work of the Western writers at the close of the nineteenth century, Perham (1936) reported that European ethnologists saw Africa as "a field for the collection of strange customs or quaint handiwork" (p. 12).

The Annang identity has been a subject of speculation by various nonnative writers who knew very little about the Annangland and its people. Messenger (1957), the first ethnographer to scientifically study the Annang of Ikot Ekpene, found the work of Talbot (1923; 1926), who wrote from Ikom and Eket, not useful in his study of the Annang and cautioned that work of colonial agents who described the people of southern Nigeria to fit colonial policies is of little use in understanding the people. Messenger further discovered that Talbot's perspective was heavily influenced by evolutionary theories of the period and individuals who served as interpreters and those who were informants to colonial agents purposely distorted information as a way to confuse those they saw as oppressors in their midst. The Europeans expected various groups in Africa to fall within distinctive and discreet boundaries. Those who failed to meet this expectation were further divided or forced to join other groups for administrative ease. As the discussion will show, some were forcibly amalgamated as punishment for rebellion or rejection of the colonial effort.

Nothing was written about the Annang group in European records until they were mentioned in connection with the slave trade in the eighteenth century in a list of slaves rescued from a slave ship on the coast of Sierra Leone. The records listed several individuals in that ship as coming from Annang and speaking the same language. Languages from other individuals on the ship not recognized by the British soldiers were so named (Udo, 1983). Thus, the group referred to themselves as such and preferred their language to be so named. Another mention of the group in European records is in connection with the Ikot Udobong Wars. King Jaja of Opobo sent in his warriors to fight with the Annang, who refused to obey his orders of not selling palm oil directly to the Efik traders. King Jaja wanted all trade with the Europeans to pass through him and wanted to maintain a monopoly of the palm oil trade.

The Annang who did not recognize the authority of the king refused to obey such orders. They insisted on being recognized as an independent nation and therefore maintained the right to trade with whoever they pleased. In the war that ensued, many of the Annangs died. The Annangs therefore sought the help of the British traders and with that help King Jaja was captured and exiled to the West Indies.

The early history of the Annangs is from oral traditions. It is believed that the group originated in ancient Egypt and through various wars and conquests was pushed south into the Sahara Desert. They moved across the desert and some settled in the upper West African region about 7500 BC. Remnants of the related language, according to Waddell, can be found among the Egyptians (Waddell, 1893). Other evidence of their Egyptian origin is found in the burial customs and veneration of the dead. Migration brought the groups to live among the Akan of Ghana where the name Annang means fourth son. From Ghana, the group moved eastward and settled among the Igbos before moving to southeast Nigeria. It was in what is present-day Nigeria that the group broke off and some of the group became known as Kwa and later Ibibio (Ekanem, 2002; Enang, 1982). It is believed that the group that remained and who could trace their origin to an ancestor known as Afaha took an oath of solidarity to be together and bonded to fight whatever was seen as a common enemy. Lineages were recognized and the groups organized themselves into clans based on old family origins much like their Igbo neighbors. In a group where conquests, wars, and migration were constant occurrences, longevity took an added significance for it meant that the individual was strong enough and was a good warrior capable of withstanding the hazards that had killed off others. It also meant that the elderly became the depository of the history of the group capable of transmitting to the younger generations the history and stories of the group. It was not therefore an accident that the elders in each group were given special recognition and positions of leadership.

One of the important ways of organization for the group was the food taboo (Enang, 1987). With the help of the religious leaders, each lineage selected an animal or plant that served as a totem for the group. They saw in the animal or plant a special affinity that spoke to their abilities and adopted the animal as an ally. The groups forbade it members from including the totem in its cuisine. Thus, those who traced their descent from Eka Abiakpo did not eat turtle. Among the people and in their myths, the turtle is seen as crafty, intelligent, and capable of deceiving larger animals and therefore not easily eaten by the enemy. The Abiakpo group therefore forbade its member from eating the turtle. Other Annang groups took on other taboos. Those from Afaha proper forbade its members from eating the (Nserise) squirrel. They identified with the quickness and intelligence of the animal. Other examples of clan groups and their food taboo are: Ukana, python (Asabo); Ekpenyong, albino Python (Ibom); Ikpe, snake (Uruk-Ikot); Utu, a kind of bird (Ebom); and Midim, African black bird (Nto Osung) (Enang, 1987; Messenger 1957). Contrary to what Messenger (1957) opined that the food taboo of the clans were only meat, there were other Annang clans who chose vegetables as their food taboo. Thus, Ika has sweet yam (anem) and Nto Edino has the river reed (Nyama). The food taboo was so important to the Annang that it was used as a distinguishing characteristic to locate the origin of an individual and to separate one Iman from another (Messenger, 1957). Children learned as part of the socialization process that a particular Iman are people living in a particular geographical area with a given food taboo.

The food taboo, as Messenger (1957) pointed out, is more than a totemic belief. However, the Annang still belief that eating the tabooed food in violation of this rule carries supernatural consequences including diseases and death. It was possible to recognize a member of an Annang clan based on the food taboo.

The Annang took the food taboo seriously and told stories of its origin to their children with an emphasis on the importance of maintaining the tradition. Among the Midim clan, for example, the oral tradition handed down through the generations is that an ancestor, Asung, who is now deified, founded the clan with a woman called Eka Midim. She had a son Midim who the clan is named after. Asung is said to have forbidden all of his descendants from eating the little black bird Nto Asung (literally translated as the children of Asung). As a mark of respect and reverence and on pain of death, each descendant of the Midim clan who violates this ancient order, it is believed, would sicken and die. This taboo among the people of the Midim clan becomes a sign of thanksgiving to the ancestors for the land, and as Enang (1987) observed, the people did not violate this law even during the famine that accompanied the Nigerian civil war.

By 3000 BC, the Annangs began to move north. The Abiakpo clan moved first and encountered the Igbos. They fought and drove the Igbos west. They were followed by the Ukana and then Utu, Ekpu, Ebom and Nyama, Adiasim, Afaha, Abak, Midim, Ekpenyong, and Ika clans (Messenger, 1957). As migration intensified, it was necessary to divide the new territories among the clans to avoid conflict. Thus, the Annang spread out to where they are presently located, with no one clan moving more than thirty kilometers from each other.

The location of each Annang Iman in a designated geographical area was so important that groups went to war with each other for violating territorial boundaries. The food taboo also served to locate an Iman in a designated geographical area. Those who lived in a particular territory were expected to abide by the food taboo of the area, but as the population increased, individuals who moved away from their territory to locate elsewhere carried their food taboo with them. Today it is possible to trace the migration pattern of the Annang Imans across the entire Akwa Ibom State of Nigeria. Thus, individuals who moved and established other communities even outside the Annang territory in neighboring Ibibio land took their food taboo with them because they believed a violation would result in death.

By 200 BC the group was well established in what is now Annangland and had formed alliances with their kin: Ibibio, who earlier on had left when they first arrived in what is presently Nigeria. Agriculture was also well developed and the group, after several wars, made peace and treaties with their Igbo neighbors. Religious traditions developed and a priestly class capable of divining the future took on prominence. It was this class that had political control and writing was suppressed. Ordinary scientific undertakings took on religious tones and interpretations and sacrifices to appease gods became a fixture that punctuated everyday lives. By the beginning of the first century AD, blacksmithing was a well-developed art in Annang and arts and crafts flourished. Festivals and initiations into classes of farming communities took on a greater significance. Individuals were rewarded with initiation into agricultural guilds.

The peaceful coexistence that characterized the early period of settlement among the Imans changed by the 1500s and wars for territories escalated. The political organization led by the eldest members of the clan was contaminated as the wealthy class used their wealth to gain political power. The introduction of secret societies including Ekpe and Abon gave the ruling class more ammunition and influence in the political system. The secret societies were introduced into Annang communities by traders who traveled outside of the area. Most of the societies were foreign to the Annang, but like most religious organizations they became syncretized and took on the local flavors. These secret societies serve as both the instruments of governance and as tools of the ruling class to enforce its will on the people. By the middle of the seventeenth century, wars among the Imans were at thair height as the slave trade provided an incentive for going to war. The Igbos who had earlier agreed to treatises violated those agreements at an alarming rate and launched several raids into Annang territories. Individuals captured in these wars were sent to the coast and marched through Ibibio territories to the coast at Itu, where they were sold to Efik middlemen who in turn sold them to the Europeans. These individuals were then taken to the new world and sold as slaves. At home, life was also difficult for Annang men, women, and children. The poor were sold for real or imagined debt (Waddell, 1893). Individuals who disagreed with the ruling elite also saw the slave trader. Children who disobeyed their parents as well as perceived "wayward" wives were also sold. Twin mothers met with the slave traders as taboos increased to make the religious leaders wealthy.

The destabilization of the society brought by the constant slave raids and the uncertainty of life in the area brought untold suffering and fear to the people. At home, nobody could be trusted. Women who refused advances of less well-to-do gentlemen disappeared from farms and on their way to the local stream for water. Because of all this, the society stagnated and the Annang group had to remain very vigilant. For more than two hundred years, the people lived in fear and young men were often stationed at entrances to the villages to warn villagers of approaching human raiders.

The abolition of the slave trade in the last part of the nineteenth century brought much-needed relief even though the buying and selling of individuals continued because of the need of the Aro priests in Igboland. No longer were the villages raided but other trade took over. Farmers were rewarded with the sale of their products to Igbo middlemen. Palm oil and palm kernels, products of the palm tree that grew everywhere, became very valuable. Individuals could harvest the fruits of the palm and exchange the extracted oil and seed for valuable goods from Europe. A wealthy class arose and the authority of the chiefs was greatly enhanced because of this new source of wealth. The new wealthy class took new wives and raised more children, thus increasing the population of the area. In fact, Groves (1936) described the Annangland in the early part of the twentieth century as "the most thickly populated area in the whole of the African continent apart from the Nile Valley" (p. 41). The new economy required new workers because the palm oil trade was labor intensive, and so the need to marry many wives served more than a traditional and cultural function. Many married from their neighbors in Andoni, Ibibio, and Igbo lands and because the slave raids had reduced the population some Iman, especially those who lived close to the Igbos, allowed parents to promise their female children to suitors when the female children were only infants. Pratten (2007) opined that the Annang culture was greatly influenced and developed as a result of the economic demands. When the slave trade required yams, for example, the culture valued those who could farm the crop in abundance. As palm oil and palm kernel became economic crops, the men made rules to control access using the new patriarchal ideas brought by the Europeans. Women were forbidden from climbing the tree and ownership of land was separated from that of the tree. Thus, while women could buy and own land, they could not own the palm tree. Yet women were needed for the labor-intensive extraction of the oil, and so marrying many wives was allowed and a good wife was one who could find additional women for the husband to marry or one who could pay the bride price for the husband's second or subsequent wife. The tree itself and the leaves became incorporated into the religious tradition, raising its importance and making it less accessible to women. The young palm fronds, for example, became a religious symbol. When individuals received the fresh young leaves of the plant it served as a warning and a summons, and mats made out of palm leaves became objects of sacrifice (Pratten, 2007).

The Annang still live together as Iman and even those who left could be traced using the food taboo as noted earlier. The early history of the Annang is difficult because of the lack of archival evidence, but it is possible to trace the history of the people using anecdotal evidence. It is safe to conclude that the people settled where the land was fertile and that the slave trade and the introduction of some practices affected how the people lived. In the next chapter, we shall examine how some of these practices affected the political and economic situations before the arrival of the missionaries and colonialists and what they saw on arrival.

*Chapter Two*

# Annang Social and Political Organization before Colonialism

To understand the turmoil that will follow, it is important to discuss the Annang social and political organization prior to colonization. In essence, the discussion of these two elements will allow for an insight into the Annang culture. The discussion will rely heavily on the work of Messenger (1957), who did an ethnographic study of the Annang people about fifty years after the arrival of the British in Ikot Ekpene. John Messenger met Udo Umo Ekam from Ikot Ekpene who was then a law student at Northwestern University in the United States. The relationship between Ekam and Messenger led to the selection of Annang as a field study interest (Messenger, 1957). This chapter will also borrow heavily from the story of Chief Udo Akpabio of Ukana Ikot Ntuen, who told his life story to Reverend William Groves, who in turn recorded the story as a contribution to a series on African studies (Perham, 1936). Chief Udo Akpabio led his people to fight against the invasion of the British soldiers in 1901. These two reliable reports serve as references for the present chapter. It is important to remember that at the time of the Messenger study, there were people who could recall the days before the British arrived. It is also possible, however, that Messenger's informants and participants might have romanticized and embellished the past, but there is no evidence to doubt the validity of the study or its conclusions. This chapter will present the judicial, political, and economic practices at the turn of the twentieth century as a way to familiarize the reader with what the Europeans saw on their arrival in Annangland.

## POLITICAL ORGANIZATION

Like their Igbo neighbors, kingship as practiced elsewhere was alien among the Annang people. Thus, the Annang were not organized under a sole monarch like others elsewhere in Africa. Each Iman was organized politically under a chief called Akuku. As discussed earlier, each Iman was distinguished by a common food taboo and consisted of individual villages (abié) who could trace their ancestry to a common individual. The Iman in turn was made up of villages headed by a chief (Awööñ Ichöñ). Each of the village chiefs was a member of the Akuku council. The function of the Akuku through his council included the maintenance of the Iman shrine (Icho Ipa Ichöñ) as well as setting dates for the Iman festivals (uchölö). Some Imans had as many as thirty villages (abié) and others like Adiasim had more. Where the Akuku resided had an important political significance for it was then considered a paramount village (Messenger, 1957). The Akuku title was hereditary and ran only through the male line.

The Iman shrine (Icho Ipa Ichöñ) played an important function in the life of the Iman. Village heads were consecrated before the shrine and brides were displayed in the square in front of the shrine after the fattening ceremony. Members of the superior warrior society called abié agwo (literary those who cut humans into two) were initiated in front of the shrine after they had demonstrated bravery in war by bringing home a human head. It was also before the shrine under the supervision of the Akuku that this group finalized preparations and plans before going to war. Thus, the Akuku, like all Annang leaders, had both political and religious responsibilities and functions. He looked after the spiritual welfare of the Imans by sacrificing at the Iman shrine and kept the cultural tradition as well as performed administrative and judicial duties. The system was federated with the Iman at the apex followed by the clan, the village, and the individual compounds consisting of extended families. Again, it is important to keep this in mind in order to appreciate the acculturative stress that is to come.

## THE JUDICIARY: BACKGROUND

Messenger (1957) described the Annang society as litigious. They believed in presenting grievances for adjudication based on their understanding of the community cleavages and relationships. The Annang court system before colonization expressed their cosmology and understanding of relationships between humans, material objects, and the spirit world. The Akuku and the chiefs ruled as part of a chain in the divine order. Thus, the village chief represented a link in that chain, ruling as a custodian of tradition and carrying on the wills of the ancestors. Those who have departed this life became part of the spirit world and messengers of the gods, who were in turn controlled by the Supreme Being called Awasi Iwom. With this understanding, testimonies in court were given noting the presence of not only the living but also the dead, the gods, and ultimately the Supreme Being. False testimonies and malice were easy to deal with as oaths given by traditional medicine men had the power to kill those who perjured themselves. This singular belief in the efficacy and power of the spirit world over the living was so strong that when individuals swore to tell the truth and the whole truth, the social understanding was that they understood the enormity of their claims and the consequences of telling a lie. Therefore family members begged each other not to swear falsely but to tell the truth in court even when it meant testifying against one's relative. As the narrative will show, swearing on the Bible to tell the truth was considered a joke during the colonial period. There were, however, some stories told by either the missionaries or those who attempted to convince the indigenous people that though swearing falsely does not kill, it is capable of making those who perjure themselves mentally ill. With the ban of the Iliöñ cult by the colonial government, former Iliöñ diviners added salt to an open page of the Bible to increase its efficacy. This author witnessed an accused individual swear by the Bible in 1966 by licking a pinch of common salt sprinkled on the page of the Psalms.

## COURT STRUCTURE

The highest court in the land was the Iman court called Échop Iman. It was held in the paramount village under the presidency of the Akuku. It was held only three times a year. This court was convened by the Akuku and had the village chiefs as members. It was the Supreme Court in each Annang Iman and handled appeals from the clan and village courts on matters religious and temporal. The court had the power to impose the death penalty for such crimes as murder, incest, and adultery. In the case of adultery, the death sentence was usually imposed on the man, while the woman was sentenced to a fine. If a child was born as a product of the adulterous relationship, that child was adopted and taken over as the child of the legitimate husband. A decision of the Échop Iman was carried out with immediate effect and was the end of the appeal process. Individuals condemned to death were taken away and executed accordingly with no waiting or holding period. Such deaths were not mourned and were done by the warriors in the evil forest. Other cases handled by the Échop Iman included land disputes between villages in the same Iman and succession rights as the village head.

Besides the highest court, five other courts were known: elder's court, village court, lineage court, family court, and market court. The elder's court, which was the subgroup court or clan (Échop Mbööñ) organized by villages who could trace their ancestry through a common ancestor, met as cases arose and had jurisdiction over the villages that so agreed to form the common court. The courts tried individuals for such offenses as theft of domesticated animals, palm wine, and yams. Messenger (1957) opined that the stealing of these items was considered an abomination because "they were considered principal objects of sacrifice" (p. 33). Stealing these items was not only an offense against humans but also against the ancestors because the items were considered sacred. Other offenses heard by the subgroup court included sexual relations with a widow before memorial rites were completed, sex with the mother of twins, and the violation of the food taboo of the Iman already mentioned. Cases to be heard by the subgroup court were initiated by the village chiefs from reports made by individuals that had knowledge of the offense. Thus, because of the Annang cosmology and belief that offenses affected more than the individual and extended to others like a wave in a pond, those who committed offenses were not hidden by even their own parents.

The most common of the courts that tried minor offenses was the village court (Échop Ichöñ). Individual villages had their own courts where the village head (Ntinya) presided. The court convened either in the village square or in the chief's residence and heard cases involving such crimes as theft of property not used in sacrifice. It also handled disputes involving different extended families (Épuk). Other responsibilities of this court included assault with a deadly weapon, getting a girl pregnant out of wedlock, refusal to participate in community activities, and property rights. Messenger (1957) listed other cases such as striking a parent or an elderly person, refusing to bear arms to defend the village, trespassing on sacred land, having sexual intercourse in the woods, refusing to refund the bride price after a divorce, and practicing evil magic. The court met in the mornings weekly and involved older men and women from the different extended families in the village. Individuals could initiate charges and request a hearing or the court was capable of charging individuals and initiating action from a report to the court. As indicated earlier, the concepts of social and communal guilt were taken very seriously and resulted in sacrifices in shrines as part of the resolution of the case to cleanse members of the offender's family and lineage.

The lineage court (échop épuuk) dealt with issues of character defamation and offenses against grandchildren and in-laws. Although Messenger (1957) maintained that character defamation usually did not result in litigation, the Annang took character defamation seriously and usually sought redress in lineage court. Membership consisted of elders of the houses that made up the extended families (épuuk). It was presided over by the head of the extended family. Cases in this court involved teenagers who disrespected the elders or parents and petty stealing and insubordination. Trespassing on lineage property and the property of members of the lineage was also a subject of hearing.

Échop Ikure or family court was another of the lower courts. This was organized by the heads of individual families to settle disputes among wives, co-wives, stepchildren, brothers, sisters, and other close relatives. It was presided over by the head of the family *Anyie Ikure* (literally translated the owner of the compound) and/or his older children. No fines were imposed in this court, but the guilty could be made to pay by producing an animal that was slaughtered and eaten by the entire family. Flogging was also a regular punishment.

The last court in the Annang judicial system was the market court (Échop Ula). Trading was very important for the community economy and the Annang understood the importance of peace and security in their economic prosperity. Therefore market courts served the function of dealing with disputes instantly as they occurred. This court handled issues of credit and unfair trade practices immediately and also dealt with assault, dispute over advantageous trading stalls, shoplifting, and other issues that may arise in the market. Membership in the court consisted of people appointed by the chiefs. Cases not easily resolved were sent to the village court.

Proceedings in the courts, except in the family courts on occasion, followed a similar pattern. Messenger's report of the proceedings would be better summarized here. The plaintiff stood before the members and paid a small "utterance" fee (Apoho Inua Ikö) used to buy palm wine for the members to drink after the session was concluded. This is not different from the filing fees charged by Western courts, except both the plaintiff and defendant pay the fee in the Annang court. Perhaps this was the reason the elders admonished their young to be careful in their dealings with the saying "*utitip apa mpö, uche ached apa mpö*," loosely translated as both winners are losers pay equally (Ette, 2010 p. 351). The fee having been satisfied, the plaintiff then states the grievance against the defendant in a long, uninterrupted speech. When it is done, the defendant rose, and again after paying the "utterance" fee stated his/her defense. In a session attended by Messenger, both were then questioned, first by one another and then by members of the court and elders attending. When the court itself initiated proceedings, the presiding member spoke as the plaintiff. The defendant could call on persons in the court to act as character witnesses. The presiding member maintained strict control of the hearing and did not permit anyone speaking to be interrupted, nor did he allow the principals to dwell on irrelevant matters. When he decided that enough evidence had been given, he sought the opinions of the important elders who serve as jurors. Messenger further reported that the chief serving as the president of the court then retired with his colleagues to discuss his decision, which rested in large measure on the advice rendered him. When the body returned to the courtroom, the verdict was announced by the presiding member (Messenger, 1957).

## EXTRA-JUDICIAL PROCESSES

Oath administrators and ordeal givers were always on hand should the judge and jury feel that one of the litigants was lying. The trial was then postponed until the effect of the oath could be ascertained. No such provision was available in the colonial court with the Bible as previously discussed. Messenger (1957) concluded this description by stating that "the mere fact of being confronted by one of these religious specialists was enough to induce additional evidence or evoke a statement of truth" (p. 38). Therefore the society was held together by a strong moral obligation based on a shared cosmology and understanding of justice and the consequences of violating what was seen as normal.

No discussion of this section will be complete without the mention of the various extra-judicial functions of different groups. Several societies with religious and military orientations were recognized in Annangland. Among these were Abié Agwo, Abön, Éköñ, Épo, Épe, and Nyama. The Abié Agwo as previously mentioned was a warrior society. Abön, Éköñ, Épo, and Épe served as the police force except that they claimed authority from the spirit world. The mask that they wore provided anonymity and provided a cover for abuse. The Nyama was a female fertility society. Members dedicated themselves to the fertility goddess and believed that adherence to the rules of the society allowed for fertility. Members performed female circumcision and took charge of all planning and maintenance of the fattening tradition of new brides. Membership was divinely arranged. Recruitment was through sickness interpreted as a sign of invitation to join the Nyama society.

The societies had codes of conduct for their members and infringement of the codes was not tolerated. It meant members could be ridiculed, shamed, fined, or expelled. This threat and actual punishment provided a deterrent that further ensured peace and tranquility in the land. We shall examine the clash between the colonialists and the Épo society later in this volume.

## LEGISLATIVE AND EXECUTIVE STRUCTURE

What has been discussed so far has alluded to the powers of the elders and other leaders. In essence, there was no separation of powers between the executive, legislative, and judicial branches as known in some Western democracies, but such functions were concentrated in the council. Political organizations of Annang were not markedly different from those of their neighbors the Igbos and the Ibibios (Anene, 1966; Offiong, 1991). The basic unit of the social order was the family and individuals trace their membership of the community to idib (literally translated stomach) (Ette, 2005; Offiong, 1991). Thus as Uzoigwe (2004) observed among the Igbos, the Annang villages were composed of individuals with consanguinal relationships who could trace their ancestry to a once "larger than life founding father" (p. 142). This understanding began in the family (ikude). Individuals who shared a blood relationship based on a common father belonged to and lived in a large compound (ikude) along with their wives and children, except that senior wives and those who had the means were allowed to marry other women and raise children from their husbands especially in the event of childlessness. This same-sex marriage was not known to be sexual, except that the women were often taken care of and provided for by both their male and female husbands. This is further proof that the Annang society was one that provided a lot of autonomy to its women, even giving the women the power to take wives with or without a man, though such wives were often given to men for the purpose of procreation. The compound was, however, headed by a man, his wives, and his children. At his death, the oldest male assumed the responsibility of heading his father's compound unless he was wealthy enough to move his own family away. Several compounds make up the family (épuk). Those who share a common épuk could trace their ancestry to a common father or mother. The family was headed by the eldest male assisted by other males. Several families together made up the village (abié). The governing authority of an abié was the village council made up of the heads of each extended family, presided over by a chief known as *Ntinya* (Messenger, 1957). The subregion (aluuk) or clan was made up of several villages who could, again, trace their ancestry to a common founder. Like the village, it had its own governing council made up of several Ntinyas from the related villages and headed by a chief known as *Achöñkö*. Several aluuks made up the Iman with a governing body made up of the heads of the subregions and headed by a paramount chief called *Akuku*.

Besides the judicial functions already described, each of the governing councils made laws to regulate behaviors and social and communal relationships, except that the Akuku retained the power to fix festival dates and religious observances throughout the Iman. No law from any jurisdiction had blanket powers and affected all of the Iman except that which was issued by the Akuku. The office of the Akuku and his council was respected and often carried severe penalties for violation including death. Yet the Annang did not assign a royal function to the office and did not acknowledge the Akuku as king even though the position was often hereditary.

The Akuku was more than a political figure and performed religious functions as well. It was his duty to ensure that sacrifices were made at the Iman shrine (Icho ipa ichöñ). Such religious duties ensured the health and prosperity of all in the Iman and gave the office an added respectability and recognition that the Akuku's job was sanctioned by the spirit world. Yet as Messenger (1957) again observed, the power of the Akuku was limited by the fact that the village head, Ntinya, had more responsibilities in the day-to-day functioning of the Annang society than the Akuku. It was the Ntinya who had local control over shrines of the village and through his council had more say in what immediately affected the villagers in the Annang society.

## SOCIAL AND ECONOMIC CONDITIONS

The Annang society was a polygamous society. A man was recognized as wealthy if he had more than one wife and the number of wives a man had conveyed his status in the society to others. Thus, it was not uncommon to see multiple marriages. Some of these were entered into as alliances, which conveyed freedom to the man to walk freely through other territories as an in-law in the days of the slave trade when individuals could be captured and sold. As a rule, especially among the wealthy class who had several wives, the children took the names of their mothers and not of their fathers. Such a practice allowed a man to recognize children from his multiple wives. Properties owned by a woman were distributed to her children upon her death. In the event of a divorce (a rare occurrence), the children were seen as belonging to the village of the father and not of the mother. Chief Udo Akpabio of Ikot Ntuen village, for example, told Reverend Groves, his biographer, that his mother's name was Akpabio Essien Ita of Ekpa Utong. His father's name was Udo Umo Ntuen, who was the chief of Ikot Ntuen in the Ukana clan (Groves, 1936). He lived briefly with his mother's kin in Ekpa Utong before returning to his father's village in Ikot Ntuen. It became possible to recognize a child's mother through the name. This practice that served the people well would later be rejected by the missionaries who refused to enter the mother's names as last names of converts of the church and as student names in schools. The European androcentric practice proved too hard for the missionaries to see the usefulness of a strong matriarchy. The Europeans would later condemn Annang feminine names such as Essien, Ukpong, and Akpabio in favor of anglicized names. As the advantage of formal education became recognized in the land, new pupils wishing to enroll in the mission schools had their name androgenized, thus such names as Essien, Ukpong, Umo, and Essiet, once names of females in Annang, became names of men. The introduction of Efik language as a school subject in 1933 put the nail in the coffin of Annang names. The educated class would later adopt Efik names such as Arit, Nko, and Ima for their daughters. Christian cosmology and worldviews brought additional names such as Emem, Nse Abasi, Mfon-Obong, and so on that inoculated the Annang society against past practices. We shall examine the acculturative stresses and changes that accompanied colonization later in this volume, but for now must describe the Annang social and economic structures prior to the British invasion.

Returning to the Annang social and economic structure, the village square (anwa Iluuñ) constituted the central social place in the life of the Annang. Each family also had a square located on a common land and served as the meeting place of the family (anwa épuuk). Important members of the family were buried on grounds next to the square and shelters erected to serve them in the afterlife called *ñgwommo* adorned the landscape. The young and women who died from childbirth and those whose death was ruled accidental were seldom buried in the family or village square but were instead interred in the evil forest. They constituted the bad spirits (épo afai) and were not capable of joining the other ancestors in protecting the community because of their youthfulness and the circumstances of their deaths. Messenger said this of the village square:

> There is always a continuous stream of traffic through the square during the day with people stopping to rest on their way to the market or farm and visiting with their neighbors. During the evening, elders congregate in and around the court building to talk, sing, and dance, while groups of children form at a distance to play games and recount folklores. (Messenger, 1957, p. 29)

It can then be surmised that the square served as the community's living room, providing a place for entertainment, relaxation, and fun.

One of the most frequent forms of entertainment was what was called Afiöñ. It is literally translated as "moon" and was played in the evening especially at moonlight. Young men played their drums while the young women danced. Individuals who had violated certain social norms formed the subjects of the Afiöñ songs. The community knew about infractions and delinquent behaviors from the songs and the offender became an object of ridicule and shame. Suitors from other villages met future brides at the dance and the young men who were good dancers met with the admiration of the young women.

The Annang society was not only about fun and games. It recognized hard work and had agricultural guilds in which those who were well to do could be distinguished in the society. Elaborate ceremonies announcing an entry into a guild also carried the implicit news to the society that a distinguished act and a great accomplishment had occurred.

The dignity of labor and festivals connected with agriculture in an agrarian society were demonstrated by the way the Annang society arranged its calendar. The year was divided into eighteen units to specify when the events occurred. Utut Isua was the end-of-year festivities and was celebrated when the harvesting was done and the hot December days without rain meant rest for the people. Immediately following the festivities of utut isua and afa isua the people had Ntem, which was a time to clear the bush for the next planting season. It was followed by ukum ikañ a few weeks afterward, when the dry bushes allowed fire to burn and clear the cut brushes. Picking up unburned twigs and clearing the land for planting had its own day known as Ñkañ atuuk (literally translated as charcoal on the body). The Annang had a saying that those whose only claim to fame is beauty better not be seen coming from Ñkañ atuuk (Ette, 2010). The next event was Utö that brought the relatives and married children together for planting. The head of the Ikure would usually fixed the planting day or days. A feast followed the end of the work day. A month or two after the planting, the season of tying the yam vines came. The males were often found in their farms tying the yam leaves to sticks (ndicha) while the women weeded around the yams. By March the women planted cassava and in May the corn was harvested. It was during this time that new brides were initiated into fattening houses as the need for labor decreased. Because the planting and tending season was over, the Éköoñ festival began. It was quickly followed by the Ikon festival, when wives entertained their husbands and presented them with gifts. It was an occasion for women to show appreciation to the men. Uchölö Anwa soon followed when young men and women danced and feasted. It is believed that the slaves taken to the new world patterned the Caribbean carnival after this festival.

The central festival among the Annang was the new yam festival called Uchölö Afa Élia. No yam could be harvested and eaten until the Akuku, with his council, declared that it was safe to do so. Eating the yam before this proclamation was an offense not only against the living but also the dead and Idio, the god of agriculture. The message was spread by the Achöñkö and Ntinya throughout the Iman. A day was fixed in each Iman and the festivities began when the Akuku blew the elephant tusk in front of the Iman shrine after sacrifices of thanksgiving to the gods and ancestors. Usually in the month of August, following the new yam festival, was the Mföñ festival. The Ebire festival was the women's festival. It celebrated the women's secret society and the harvest of the Ebire crop. Like the Ikon festival, wives were expected to fete the family. Nkai celebrated the old yams and provided a social occasion for celebrations and feastings. The last of the festivals was Nlök and was celebrated with cleaning things of the old year. Bereaved families went to the graves of the deceased and literally stomped on it and in the process reduced it from a mound to level ground. Utim Uli, as the event was called, provided an occasion to finalize the grieving period. By the middle of the sixteenth century when Épo was introduced, the Nlök became a time to send this representative of the spirit world into the forest. By 1901, the Épo society had taken over the Nlök festival and made it exclusively theirs.

To appreciate the change that will follow, let us turn our attention now to the Annang economic value system. The most important crop was the yam. Other farm produce, except for livestock, was seen as belonging to the female domain. Therefore the society had guilds in which those who produced the most crops through hard work could be recognized. Although Messenger (1957) maintained that the Annang looked down on titles and did not recognized titles from other places, it did not mean that the Annang Iman hated titles. The Annang guarded their identity and because experience had taught them the importance of holding on to their identity they refused to recognize titles outside Annang Iman as a way of exerting their independence.

Three titles that suggested class were recognized and conferred by the Annang regardless of gender. The first one was Idio, named after the god of agriculture. Individuals who had acquired a rack of yams (iche) could assume the title after it was ascertained that such and individual or individuals were people of good moral character. The route to wealth was as important as the wealth itself. Thus, individuals with questionable character could not assume the title no matter the quantity of yam. Only an Idio or one who is higher could confer the title after the festivities. More racks were celebrated with feasting until twenty-one racks were acquired, at which time the Idio took on a new titled called Énañ. As with the Idio title only those who had taken the Énañ title could confer it to a new initiate. Days of festivities accompanied the conferring of the title. The highest title among the Annang was the Inam title. Forty-nine racks of yam were required. Individuals had to be people of good moral character. The achievement of the Inam title brought days and even weeks of feasting and celebrations. It should be mentioned here that children born to these title holders during the time of the festivities took the titles as their last names instead of the normal assumption of the mother's first name that was the custom. Thus, it was possible to have Apan (Apa) Idio, Apan (Apa) Enang, Apan (Apa) Inam, or Udo Enang, Udo Inam, or Udo Idio, all denoting the order of birth to the celebrant.

The Annang social, political, and economic systems served the people for generations and revolved around a basic value of respect for the elders, living or dead. Violations were not tolerated and were seen within the worldview as affecting the entire community. Sanctions were quick. Hard work was rewarded. The Annang in the words of Chinua Achebe (1959) were not in one long night of savagery where the Europeans acting on God's behalf delivered them. They had their institutions and were aware of others around them. They fought wars to protect their identity and were guided by traditions, history, and values that had guided and preserved them for generations.

Pratten (2007) opined that the Annang economic activities and culture were affected by events in the international community. In the height of the slave trade, yam became an important cash crop because the slave ships used it during the transatlantic voyage. This big demand created a huge market for the crop. With the abolition of the inhuman trade and a new use for palm oil, the product gained importance and the Annang men established new rules that further destroyed the matriarchal system of the Annang society.

## RELIGION AND BELIEFS

Perham (1936) made an interesting observation about European knowledge of Africans. Despite controlling the destinies of tens of millions of people, she opined that very little was understood of the people. To fill this void, she continued, the Europeans

> make do with assumptions; the primary one, that Africans are backward; next that they are inherently, and so permanently backward . . . we think of them or deal with them in the mass, according to our various standpoints, as "natives" or the "native problem," as the heathen; as hut and poll tax payers, or as "native labour." We see the strange, stupid or cruel things they do and ignorant of their motives. (Perham, 1936, p. 3)

The Annang religion was one such strange thing to the Europeans. Like all societies, the Annang had an understanding of the world that fulfilled their needs and conveyed meaning to life and existence, for as Durkheim (1912) reminded us, religion fulfills a need and satisfies certain aspects of life. As noted earlier, the Annang traditional religion involved a belief in a Supreme Being called *Awachi Anyöñ* who was powerful, transcendent, immanent, and omniscient. Because of these attributes God worked in the world through intermediaries. These were spirits and gods. Awachi Anyöñ created the world but handed over the responsibilities of its functioning to various gods who act as messengers. Each physical creation and human endeavor has an assigned god who must be obeyed and sometimes pacified. The gods receive sacrifice on behalf of the Supreme Being. The ancestors are part of the pantheon and intercede on behalf of the living. They serve as intermediaries between the world of the living and the spirits, therefore dishonoring the ancestors or not properly burying the dead can affect such intercession. A favorite saying among the Annang is that those who owe the dead are the ones who are afraid of noises in the dark for it is believed that the dead can return and ask for proper burial and remembrance. There is also a belief in evil spirits called mbiam (Ekanem, 2002). These messengers of the gods can be summoned for diabolical purposes including harming one's enemies causing illness and death. Those who lie or engage in criminal activity, including murder, were made to swear on mbiam.

The Annang believed that certain gods were in charge of certain aspects of life meant only for the initiates. Guilds and membership organizations and secret societies of various kinds belonged in this category. Members devoted themselves to secret meetings. Membership in some secret societies and organizations was through a call. Individuals through illness or some divine revelation joined such organizations and swore allegiance and participated in the society. One of such society was the Éponyöñ cult. Members were often initiated into the secret society at adolescence, after the loss of a child, or after recovering from an illness. They were informed by the Iliöñ Priest that they were called to be a member of such a secret society. Those so initiated changed their name to Inyañ and were required to bring a jar of water from the river to their home. The Mami Wata cult is a syncretic practice of this ancient secret society when European traders joined with the belief that it would prevent them from the treacherous ocean journey. The introduction of the mermaid European myth has led some to opine that Mami Watta was introduced from Europe or America into Africa rather than the other way round.

Another confusion with the Annang belief system has to do with witchcraft. This European ancient secret society is not indigenous to Africa and was introduced by European traders to those who lived near the coast. Witchcraft is a moon cult of Western European pagan religion (Gardener, 1959). The practice was not widespread among the Annang due to their late association with the Europeans. Items of sacrifice used in witchcraft are clearly foreign. The Annang do not use foreign foods to sacrifice to their deities. The abundant cassava crop, for example, a food item imported from South America and the Caribbean by the returnees in the eighteenth century, is not used as an item of sacrifice among the Annang. Similarly, rice, stew, beer, and soda, all imported foreign food items used by witches as items of sacrifice, cannot be used for the indigenous gods. Therefore Ekanem (2002) was wrong to see witchcraft as an indigenous Annang secret society.

The Annang religion may be called Iliöñ. Though there was no sacred text, the Iliöñ priest performed the sacrifices on behalf of the people and divined the future. They had enormous power and prescribed the moral code. They knew when a sacrifice was needed and what kind was needed. They considered themselves called by the gods to serve on behalf of the people and were well respected. A call required a period of apprenticeship, but by the late nineteenth century, corruption had set in and the British colonial authorities and missionaries would accuse the members of this guild of the gruesome murders of the early twentieth century (Pratten, 2007).

## HEALTH AND HEALTHCARE

The link between religion and healthcare was not far off but neither was it intertwined. It is true that the source of illness, especially if such illness was major, was located either in the realm of the spirit or from a supernatural criminal, often a relative who is jealous and has brought a calamity to the individual through supernatural means (Offiong, 1991). Other etiologies of illnesses include the violation of sacred places and laws. Common illnesses were known such as cold, stomachache, and malaria and were often treated with local herbs and roots within the home, while severe illnesses were referred to experts outside of the home depending on how such illness was perceived. Accidents and illnesses suspected of having natural causes, including broken bones, were sent to the experts. Because those individuals from Abiakpo clan (literally bone experts) were said to descend from an individual who worked on healing bones, the Annang believed her descendants could cure broken bones. Illnesses with supernatural etiologies such as punishments from past lives (*ésién émana*), mental illness, or those not well understood or rare brought in supernatural healers. We have already seen that the Iliöñ cult played a critical role in the Annang culture. The Annang help-seeking behavior was not different from other humans in the world. The first action in this pattern was to try self-healing then reach out to those who are close until the circles widen to include experts. The use of herbs and roots is proof that there was separation between religion and medicine.

In this chapter, we have explored the social and political world of the Annang before the arrival of the colonialists and have argued that the society had its laws, rules, and system of governance. We have further explored the economic and social structures, arguing in the process that what the people practiced reflected their understanding of their social world and learned meanings to their place in the universe. In the next chapter we will examine the advent of colonialism and seek to show its effects on the people.

## Chapter Three

# British Colonialism

The literature is replete with the activities of British colonial administration in Africa and it is equally active with the activities of the missionaries. There were, however, three different contacts with the Europeans and for our purposes it is necessary to divide them into their proper roles: the traders, the missionaries, and the colonialists (Ette, 2001). Many African scholars have written about the missionaries and have divided themselves into two camps: those who see the missionaries as benefactors and those who vilify them. As written about elsewhere, no serious scholar of African history can afford to ignore the missionaries for they provided a tool and a map for the colonization enterprise (Ette, 2001; Nwaka, 1986; Hardage, 2002; Ekanem, 2002). For the Annang, however, the activities of the European missionaries and British colonizers reflected earlier beliefs about the savagery of those the European traders referred to as Egbo Sharry. The name Egbo Sharry was a corruption of two Efik terms, Ekpo Iseri, and translates as the proud poor. It was a derogatory name given by the Efiks to those who lived away from the coast. Because the Efiks, who are related to the Annangs, lived in the coastal areas and traded with the Europeans, they became wealthy and also saw themselves as more civilized according to the evolutionary ideas of the time. They could acquire articles of trade and materials from international maritime traders and borrowed even the dressing of those they traded with. Some like Antera (Antigha) Duke (1785) could even learn to read and write and also kept personal diaries in the eighteenth century. The refusal of those in the hinterland to recognize the economic dominance of the Efiks and the pride of belonging to the old ancestral land by the Annang and Ibibio earned them the term "Ekpo Iseri." The Efiks originally migrated from the Ibibio area in Uruan to Calabar.

Let us return to the story of the invasion of Annangland by the British forces. The invasion of the British soldiers in 1901 was a shock that dramatically changed the society forever. This chapter will attempt to describe the European entry into what is now southeast Nigeria. It will attempt to separate the Europeans into their proper roles. The underlying argument is that though the roles were separate, the Europeans worked together for the domination of the African society. In order to fully understand the Annang history, let us now locate it within the Nigerian political history.

On January 8, 1897, a young British reporter named Flora Shaw, engaged to Frederick Lugard, who later became the first governor general of Nigeria, wrote a report in the *London Times* about the Royal Niger Company Territories on her return from Africa. Finding the designation Royal Niger Territories "inconvenient" and "misleading," she wrote:

> it may be possible to coin a shorter title for the conglomeration of Pagan and Mohammedan States . . . brought by the exertions of the company within the confines of a protectorate and thus need for the first time in its history to be described as an entity . . . the name "Nigeria" applying to no other nation of Africa may without offence to any neighbours be accepted. (*The Times of London*, January 8, 1897, p. 6; quoted in Ette, 2010)

Thus, for want of a better name, this West African country larger than Great Britain was named and today is known by the name given to it by the wife of its first governor. It became a colony of Great Britain in the words of Frederick Forsyth (1969) when "it had not been conquered; it had not really been explored. It had no name, so Lady Lugard gave it one—Nigeria" (p. 13). In June 1898, the Anglo-French agreement established the borders of present-day Nigeria with Niger, the former French colony in the north, the Atlantic Ocean in the south, the Benin Republic in the west, and Cameroon in the east.

Thus, the Annangs were assigned to a country without their consent and had no knowledge that the Igbos, the Efiks, the Ibibios and the Andonis—their neighbors that they had been at war with at various times—were now fellow citizens of a country whose name they did not yet know when they were invaded in 1901. It took a few more years before the Annangs knew that their society had changed.

## EUROPEAN TRADERS

Though the Annang had very little contact with the Europeans, the latter had extensive contact with other indigenous groups in southeast Nigeria, notably the Efik who lived on the Cross River tributaries of the Atlantic Ocean. As early as the sixteenth century, the Portuguese traded with the people of the coastal areas and later the British slave ships carried captured humans to the Americas from the Calabar coast. Because the Annang live less than one hundred miles from the Efiks in Calabar where the British invasion was launched, it is important to begin the analysis by providing a historical background of the Efiks' contact with the Europeans.

European contact at Calabar at first did not alter the Efik economic and social organization. They continued to fish and sell their catches to those who lived up the river until the Europeans arrived with their ships in the middle of the seventeenth century and the demand for slaves and palm oil led to a radical change not only in the fabric of the society but also in ethical and moral relationships. Waddell (1863) and Forde (1956) noted that the European traders were fleeting visitors. They anchored in the river long enough to obtain their cargo and left as soon as that was accomplished. They had no interest or desire to learn the Efik language and, motivated by profit and racism, they exploited the people for their gain.

Talbot (1926) reported that the name Calabar or Old Calabar is not shown on fifteenth- or sixteenth-century Spanish and Portuguese maps but first appeared on Dutch maps of the sixteenth century. The earliest record of trade with Calabar is recorded by a ship captain, John Watts. In a record of the ship, *Peach Tree* of London, in 1668, Mr. Watts wrote that the *Peach Tree* "sailed to Old Calabar in the Bay of Guiney" (quoted in Latham, 1973). By 1672 many ships went there to carry slaves and ivory. By 1700, as the demand for slaves to work the plantations in the newly discovered American continents rose, the Dutch, French, Portuguese, and English were competing with each other and the traffic in human cargo could not keep up with the demand (Latham, 1973). Antera (Antigha) Duke (1785), a native of Calabar who kept a personal diary at this time, listed the number of people taken away into the ships as slaves for several months.

The slave trade changed the Calabar society. The European traders utilized the trust system whereby the locals would be given articles of trade in exchange for a future delivery of slaves (Duke, 1785) Failure to deliver the expected number of slaves and articles led to personal danger and intimidation (Waddell, 1863). This led to pressure to fulfill expectation and obligations. The arms for slave raids were provided by the ships. Strong liquor was introduced into the society. In 1750, John Newton, who would later leave his career as a slave ship captain and pen the Christian hymn *Amazing Grace*, wrote:

> strong liquor being an article much in demand, without it scarcely a single slave can be purchased, it is always at hand. And if what is taken from the casks or

bottles that are for sale be supplied with water they are as full as they were before. The blacks, who buy the liquor are the losers by the adulteration. (Newton, 1750)

Pressure to deliver led to inhumane practices. Isaac Parker, who jumped ship and spent five months in Calabar, described a raid he participated in 1765 before the British House of Commons thus: "Armed with weapons the party waited in the bushes in the day and captured and handcuffed all they could see at the edge of the village. Forty-five people were thus forcefully taken away and sold over to the ships. The raid was repeated again two weeks afterwards" (Imbua, 2013). Between 1785 and 1788, Antera Duke recorded in his private diary that 7,511 people were taken away by the ships in Calabar, while the ship records in Liverpool recorded 2,810 in 1752, 3,050 in 1771, 2,473 in 1798, and 1,654 in 1799 (Simmons, 1956). It is important to keep this in mind in order to appreciate the contribution of the Christian missionaries who would later preach against this inhuman practice. Waddell (1863) noted that the traders and missionaries were often divided on matters of religion and morality and he described the traders as "the greatest hindrance to the spread of the gospel in the coast of Africa." In a letter to Dr. David Jennings in August 1752, John Newton described the workers on his slave ship thus:

> We are for the most part supplied with the refuse and dregs of the nation. The prisons and the glasshouse furnished us with large quotas and boys impatient of their parents and masters, or already ruined by some untimely vice and for the most part devoid of all good principles. (Newton, 1750, p. 107)

The ships therefore were notorious for rapes of the local women and the slaves.

The trade method was barter, and in addition to the goods exchanged, each ship had to pay a duty known as "Comey" to the local rulers (perhaps a short form of the word "commission"). The quantity and acceptable goods for the "comey" were regulated by the tonnage of the ship. Though copper bars and rods were used as means of exchange, barter continued to be an acceptable form of payment.

The value of written records was recognized by the Efik traders and some of them were effectively instructed in writing and keeping records by the ships. Several European accounts and journals refer to the keeping of accounts at this time. Adams (1823) reported that there were schools in Calabar for the children of the wealthy traders and that some of their children had visited England. Antera (Antigha) Duke kept a personal diary and King Eyo Honesty II himself helped the missionaries to interpret their sermons to the people.

## MISSIONARY ACTIVITIES

Another contact with the Europeans with a lasting impact was through the activities of the Christian missionaries. Many historians have written on the reasons that the Christian missionaries went to Calabar (Aye, 1987; Ayandele, 1966). It is impossible to speak of the Christian mission to Calabar without giving credit to the Africans who lived in Jamaica. On gaining their freedom, these Africans who were sold as slaves remembered their former homes and wished to impart to those not familiar with the gospel message in their homeland the benefits of the Christian religion. Waddell (1863) reported that freed slaves in Jamaica, though very poor themselves, gave generously to the African mission.

Several events led to the arrival of the Christian missionaries on the shores of Calabar. While the Africans in Jamaica were working on sponsoring a Christian mission to Calabar, a British war ship commanded by Commander Raymond signed a treaty with Calabar kings and chiefs for the abolition of the slave trade and spoke with them about the need to receive Christian missionaries. Captain Beecroft, who was stationed at Fernado Po, a vacation island and rest home for Efik kings, persuaded the kings to accept missionaries and outlined the advantages of such an endeavor in education, trade, and eventual wealth. In a letter written by King Eyo Honesty II to Commander Raymond dated December 1, 1842, the king wrote:

> I am glad you come and settle treaty proper, and thank you for doing everything right for me yesterday. Long time I look for some Man-of-War and when French man come I think he want war and send one canoe to let you know . . . no one come help me keep treaty as Mr. Blount promise and when I no give slaves French Man-of-War come make plenty palaver. . . . One thing I want for beg your queen, I have too much man now, I can't sell slaves I don't know what to do for them. But if I can get some cotton and coffee to grow, and man for teach me, and make sugar cane for we country come up proper, and sell for trade side I very glad. Mr. Blyth tell me England glad for send man to teach book and make we understand God all same white man do. If queen do so I glad too much, and we must try do good for England always. (Quoted in Waddell, 1863, p. 664)

Aye (1987) deduced from the foregoing that the reasons for the invitation to the missionaries were for "the development of agriculture, of trade and of Christian education and evangelism." The king was only interested in the Christian religion insofar as it could provide the knowledge needed for agriculture and the advancement of learning. It may even be concluded that because of the Efik worldview of a divine influence in all matters, the king believed that the European religion was an essential part of the ability to acquire Western education and technology. Waddell noted in his private journal a conversation that he had with King Eyo. The king told Reverend Waddell in 1846, "a school in our town to teach our children to saby book like white people will be very good thing" (quoted in Nair, 1972, p. 87). The abolition of the slave trade had seriously affected the economic situations of the kings and chiefs. The vacuum created by the abolition required that something else take its place. The threats from the French in their efforts to acquire colonies and slaves were very real to the kings. Throughout most of recorded history, it has been "human nature" for individuals to seek protection from others when life has been uncertain and the future bleak. It is a survival technique in the midst of a decaying hope to work to improve the future picture when it appears uncertain, and so the kings, having heard so much about the advantages of having missionaries, requested that these church workers, which they perhaps thought of as miracle workers, be sent to live among them.

Many Europeans at the time following abolition felt a sense of obligation to help a continent that they had participated in wronging. Mr. Ferguson, for example, who had served as a surgeon in a slave ship until 1832, donated one thousand pounds when he learned of the Calabar Mission Movement in Jamaica (Livingstone, 1916). Reverend Anderson, who was the early pioneer of the Calabar mission, in a speech before the annual meeting of the missionary board, reminded his fellow Christians:

> How many cargoes of slaves have been carried down from the Old Calabar River, in British ships, to British colonies, there to toil, on, on, on, no rest in prospect but the grave for the enriching of British subjects? Britain's guilt and Africa's wrong—neither the one nor the other can be cancelled till, in return for the injuries inflicted on poor Africa, she be put, by Britons in possession of the best blessings. (Quoted in Marwick, 1897, p. 367)

Others not affiliated with the church supported the missionaries in the hope that the Africans would be taught other economic activities. The expectation was that it would check the slave trade at its source and eliminate organized raids on defenseless people that were eventually sold for the wealth and gain of the powerful in the society.

When the slave trade was finally abolished, former slaves who were taken away to Jamaica bonded together and contributed whatever they could to send a missionary to teach the people they left behind the message of the Christian Gospel. Reverend Hope Waddell serving then in Jamaica as a missionary of the Scottish Missionary Society was impressed with the efforts of these poor former slaves who themselves had very little. He communicated this information to his superiors in Edinburgh, Scotland, and volunteered to go to Calabar as a missionary to the Africans (Waddell, 1863). Despite being discouraged by the mother church in Scotland, who saw such adventure as "premature and displaying more zeal than judgment not accordant with the state of dependence in which the Jamaica church stood" (p. 208), these former slaves along with their Scottish missionaries pressed on.

As Falola (1998) observed, it is ironic that the abolition of the slave trade contributed to the successful planting of Christianity in Nigeria in particular and Africa in general. It is equally ironic that very little credit is given to former slaves in the literature about these individuals who helped in the Christian mission in Africa. Previous attempts by the Europeans to introduce the religion in the fifteenth century failed, and by the eighteenth century the Portuguese missionaries who led the effort in Benin and Warri abandoned the idea (Groves, 1948). By the mid-nineteenth century, former slaves in Jamaica and elsewhere contributed money and traveled to Africa to work as missionary agents. They could withstand the climate, helped as interpreters, and worked in the construction of homes and schools, and many died and were buried in the homeland.

In 1843 the Calabar chiefs, desperate for trading and business to replace the slave trade that had been banned by Britain, sent a letter to Scotland asking for Europeans to come and live among them to teach them new trades. In fact, the letter assured the Europeans that a parcel of land had already been donated for use by those who would be sent to them (Waddell, 1863).

Motivated by economic interest and the threats of war by British naval officers, the Efik kings looked for other ways of alliances with Britain. With a little encouragement from Captain Beecroft, who was stationed at Fernado Po as the governor of that Island, the Efik kings not only agreed to allow the missionaries in but also gave the tract of land free to the new mission. The missionaries arrived in 1846 in Calabar and there began the relationship between Britons and Nigerians in the southeast that would have lasting impact on all who live in the area.

Waddell, Edgerly, their wives, and other Africans from Jamaica who accompanied them on the journey set out to work among the Efiks. In earlier times, the Efiks did not allow the European traders to leave their ships and therefore imposed themselves as middlemen in the trade with the Europeans; however, no such restriction was imposed on the new arrivals. The agreement of the Efik chiefs to allow the Church Missionary Societies missionaries to move freely was an admission that things have changed. They accepted the missionaries to live among them without taxes because they needed their expertise. In fact, when Mr. Jameson died early in the mission project, the people of Calabar were afraid that other surviving members would leave. In a letter of condolence written to Reverend Hope Waddell (1863) by the son of Eyo Honesty II, the prince wrote:

> My dear Master and Friend,
> 
> I am too sorry about your brother, Mr. Jameson, died, and I hope you will not go away, leave us, because God been give us good friend, and take him away again. We cannot [know] why he do this, but I am very sorry. I hope God will keep you well to us, to stop and teach we all know him.
> 
> With best compliments, I am your friend, Y. Eyo HTY (Waddell, 1863, p. 344)

## THE COLONIAL ENTERPRISE

Beattie (1953) noted that no serious social study of African development and modern history could afford to neglect the Christian missionary. This assertion is still true today and no good story of African development can gloss over the story of Christian evangelization. The proper role of the Christian missionary in Africa, as already noted, is at best murky for the missionary was both a representative of a particular denomination as well as a citizen and member of a particular country and time. As an agent of a religious organization, they had a duty to spread and establish the faith, but as citizens of their individual countries they felt a sense of patriotism to support their government. As those who live in a particular time they were also driven by the worldviews of their time. Thus, stories abound of the duplicity of the Christian missionaries with colonialism. Many of the missionaries made no apologies and had very little illusion that their goal with the colonial enterprise aligned. According to Reverend Boer (1988) of the Sudan United Mission:

> Colonialism is a form of imperialism based on a divine mandate and designed to bring liberation—spiritual, cultural, economic and political—by sharing the blessings of the Christ-inspired civilization of the west with a people suffering under satanic forces of oppression, ignorance and disease, effected by a combination of political, economic and religious forces that cooperate under a regime seeking the benefit of both ruler and ruled. (Quoted in Falola, 1998, p. 33)

Among the Efiks, on the other hand, the struggle with colonial agents was already present when the Church Missionary Societies missionaries arrived in Calabar in 1846. The British navy patrolling the tributaries and the bight of Biafra already had agents in the Island of Fernado Po, a land regarded as the vacation homes of the Calabar elites before the colonialists arrived and therefore part of Calabar. The French on the other hand, desirous of colonies, had their navy in the area too, as did the Spaniards. Waddell (1863) told a story about an encounter with the French navy and the role of the missionaries in ensuring that Calabar remained in British hands.

With intelligence report from unnamed sources, Waddell learned that two French war ships were approaching the Calabar coast. The mission of the troop was to get a treaty signed by the Calabar chiefs that would have made Calabar a French colony. Knowing the implication of such a treaty on their work, the missionary quickly sent word to the ruling class in the Calabar areas, warning them of the impending arrival of the French troops and advising them to be on guard. With fear planted in the minds of the people about the uncertainty and designs of the French, the king of Duke Town sent a letter to Reverend Hope Waddell ensuring him of his unwillingness to sign any treaty with the French. Chief Young wrote:

> I hear news about the French man-of-war want to come here for make we put hand for book to them for take country. That is what I never been here since my grandfather be. But I will do no such thing. I must see you before that come. (Waddell, 1863, p. 350)

The following day, Reverend Waddell himself was present as the French met with the kings and made sure that the kings flew the Union Jack in their houses before going to the meeting. The missionary also met privately with the king before he honored the French invitation to their ship. King Eyo, perhaps as a result of the meeting with the missionary, insisted on flying the English flag on his canoe to meet the French. As a result of the work and prodding of Reverend Waddell, the Efik chiefs did not sign the treaty with the French.

With the missionaries in the area, Britain proceeded to the business of pacifying and controlling the area. When Britain firmly took control of what is now Nigeria, they divided the country into two protectorates: northern and southern. Sir Ralph Moore was appointed the high commissioner of the south. Unlike the north, the south lacked a caliphate-type administration and most ethnic groups in the south were autonomous and independent political entities who looked at outsiders with suspicion and mistrust. Therefore the southerners, in what is today the southeast of Nigeria, did not accept colonialism easily. British influence therefore was mostly in the western part of Nigeria, the area around Calabar, and the northern part of the country. As Livingstone (1916) observed, "there were still large stretches practically untouched by the agents of the government, including the territory lying between the Cross River and the Niger" (p. 177). Life in these territories continued like it had for many centuries. If the colonial enterprise was to succeed, all the ethnic groups needed to be brought into the control and influence of the colonialist, and so it became necessary to plan for the enforcement of British rule and domination of the people.

The reason given for the planned expedition was to enforce the abolition of slavery and to stop human sacrifice in the Long Juju shrines of Arochukwu and therefore stop the demand for slaves that were needed for the sacrifices. Behind this stated and manifest goal was the pacification of the people and a forced annexation into colonial British control.

## THE LONG JUJU OF AROCHUKWU

The Aros were notoriously resistant to British rule. Stories of the Aro brutalities along with their resisting the incursion of the missionaries into their territories infuriated the colonial authorities in Calabar. Like Hope Waddell before her, Mary Slessor, once a missionary and later a colonial agent, heard several reports about the Aro and transmitted those reports to her superiors. The missionaries saw the resistant of the Aros and their neighbors as standing in the way of spreading enlightenment to those they considered heathens. When the plan to send in an expedition force was hatched, the missionaries joined in and dispatched one of their own, Dr. Rattray, who was the mission's physician, to join as a medical officer in the expedition (Livingstone, 1916).

The Long Juju of Arochukwu was a fierce and much-feared deity worshipped by the Igbos. Its influence was felt all over the land between the Cross River and the Niger because of the demand for human sacrifice needed to appease the god. Such demand required waging war on neighboring groups to secure humans for this purpose. Livingstone (1916) reported that the priests of the Aro god had become so corrupt that they waged wars in the name of their god in order to get slaves to sell for their own benefit. For this reason, the Aro blocked trade routes and resisted the authority of the British colonial government. The Long Juju itself was located in a secret gorge that was guarded. The priests made money from individuals who traveled long distances to consult their god. Mysterious deaths and unexplained events required that the individuals go to the Aros to consult their god who knew the future and could predict human events.

The priests of the Long Juju were regarded as having mysterious powers bestowed on them by their god. The shrine itself was built in the middle of a stream where fish abound because fishing was not permitted. The color of blood in the water meant someone had been sacrificed and the sacrifice was accepted by the god. Individuals who entered the shrine and were known to have lied were devoured by the god. The color of blood in the water was an indication that such individuals were taken by the Long Juju.

One aspect of this religion would have serious implications for the Annang in 1901. The Long Juju priests had agreements and relationships beyond the

Igbo area. They had orders and a secret society in which members swore blood brotherhood (Livingstone, 1916). Members had obligations to protect each other and to serve the interests of those who have sworn allegiance to this brotherhood. Through this network, the slave system was sustained and perpetuated. It was the abolition of the slave trade and the opening of the trade and mission routes that prompted the "expedition" of the territories west of the Cross River, as already noted.

In this chapter we have briefly traced the British contact with people in southeast Nigeria and have argued that these contacts worked in unison for the defeat of the African mind. More importantly, this brief sketch has laid the background in understanding what is to follow and a brief narrative as a way to locate the Annang within the Nigerian history. The British invasion of Annangland was not done out of benevolence but was necessitated by the need to open up the hinterland to British rule. The British had heard for centuries about the savages of the Egbo Sharry country, as they called the inhabitants of this interior. Stories of cannibalism and primitive practices abound and so armed with fear and ignorance, they mobilized forces to pacify these primitive tribes as they saw them.

*Chapter Four*

# The Invasion of Annangland

Unlike other groups in Nigeria, the Annang contact with the Europeans can be described as shock and awe. While their kin and neighbors like the Efiks had a peaceful introduction predicated upon trade and Christian evangelism, the Annang were forced at gunpoint to accept colonialism or die. The Annang reputation as bellicose in nature did not help matters. Throughout the territories of the period, the Annangs were noted for their charms and expertise in the use of the machete and had warrior societies that members distinguished themselves in the severance of the heads of the enemy called Abie Awo (Messenger, 1957). This chapter will examine the arrival of the British force in Ikot Ekpene, the Annang cultural capital, as the beginning point of Annang colonialism and will attempt to show the effects of that arrival on the Annang tradition, culture, and identity.

Before we begin the examination of the invasion, it is perhaps important to discuss the factors that led to the event itself. Livingstone (1916) provided the rationale for the military expedition as being necessary "to break up the slave system and the false gods of the Aro" (p. 193). Therefore, as we saw already, two forces were at work in the events that led up to the invasion. First, the Christian missionaries saw the superstitions of the hinterland as standing in the way of the spread of the Gospel, and therefore they saw the British military as an answer to the stubbornness of the people. Second, the slave system that continued to flourish despite British laws required a military response to break the powers of the Aro priests and blood brotherhood. Historians have long recognized the twin forces in African colonialism, namely the Bible and the crown, and this was not different. But beyond these mundane reasons lie the philosophical. As Waugh (1894) observed, the activities of nations "[show] its people its natural face in a glass and leaves to posterity the record of the manner of man it found." The individuals who organized the Aro expedition were those who believed in the philosophy that guided the Victorian age. They were products of Victorian intellectualism and education. They were from an age that believed in the philosophical current of the time known as Realism (Decker, 1952). They believed in the philosophy that there was an objective world out there waiting to be discovered and it was the duty of the "civilized" to teach the heathens and those whose development had been arrested the ways of truth. It was this later belief, interpreted as "Christian duty," that united the missionaries with the colonialists and set the stage for the invasion of Annangland and similar places in Africa. As Barrett (1968) observed, the Africans were considered barbarians who had to be protected from themselves. The colonialists saw themselves as members of a superior race destined to rule. In fact, Livingstone (1916) described the war that ensued in the hinterland as "the forces of civilization encounter(ing) the warriors of barbarism" (p. 193). And so, he continued, "punitive expedition" had to be organized. Therefore, besides opening up the interior for British rule and missionary enterprise, the expedition was designed to punish and inflict casualties on any group that dared challenged the hegemony and superiority of those destined to conquer, especially those that the British saw as primitive and backward. With a clear justification and separation of good versus evil in the minds of the invaders, the brutality that followed changed the Annang society forever.

## THE COMING OF THE STORM

The Annang believe that certain events occur in the community to serve as a warning or harbinger of greater things to come and they express this beautifully in their proverb "*Éto ama atö agwo itak utöñ annö item*" (meaning a stick hitting the ear is a call to listen to counsel). And so certain historical events were reexamined after the fact as forewarnings of what they were then experiencing.

About 1880, much of the agricultural products of the Annang were destroyed by locusts. This pest was a source of worry for the Annang and whenever it appeared, the people saw it as a bad sign that a great evil was about to befall them. Because locust usually destroyed the farmlands, starvation was common following an invasion. What was different then was that the locust invasion was quickly followed by the smallpox (mfat Ito) epidemic. Many people died from this disease, including warriors responsible for the defense of the society. The two events occurring quickly in sequence raised the alarm of all the religious leaders (Mbia Iliöñ) in the whole of Annangland. Many clans and Iman prepared for war and young men were required to be vigilant. As already mentioned, clashes with the neighbors were common and the events were interpreted as signs that something serious was coming. Something bad did happen beyond the imagination of the people.

As mentioned earlier, Sir Ralph Moore was appointed high commissioner for the southern protectorate of Nigeria and was stationed in Calabar. The administration of the south, unlike the northern part of Nigeria, was made difficult by the inaccessibility of the hinterland between the Cross River and the Niger River. Reports of continuing trade in humans in the hinterland, especially among the Aros, were known by the Europeans in Calabar. Another reason for the European entry into the hinterland, according to Messenger (1957), was the need to open up the interior for direct trade with the Europeans after the British Parliament had made the slave trade illegal. When the slave trade was legal, there was no need to enter into the interior because the African middlemen made slaves available on the coast without any risk to the European traders. With the abolition of the slave trade, other articles of value needed to be discovered. It was therefore important that the expedition be organized to open up the hinterland. The soldiers were sent from Calabar and ordered to the Enyong Creek. From there they advanced, burning down huts and shooting at any real or imagined resistance. The commander of the British invasion force was Colonel Montanaro, a no-nonsense Victorian career military officer who believed in the divine destiny of the white man and the duty of spreading the protestant faith as a way of saving the heathens (Livingstone, 1916). When the troop reached Arochukwu, they burned the Long Juju shrine, captured and killed many of the priests, and destroyed the villages connected with the worship of the god. Some escaped and disappeared into the secret network of the blood brotherhood that was mentioned earlier. Despite fierce resistance, the Aros were easily defeated.

What happened in Arochukwu did not escape the notice of the Annang who were trading partners of the Aro. Some of the Annang had initiated in the blood brotherhood of the Aro and were friendly to some of the priests. Stories of strange white-looking people who kill and burn houses were told in village squares in Annangland. Many who heard these stories believed that the Annang could mount better defenses than the Aros and many chiefs readied their troops in case of an attack. Some did believe that the invaders would never reach Annang becuase the Annang had a solid reputation for bravery and were known for their charms. Because of the centrality and importance of Annang, the Aro established settlements in some Annang areas where they bought slaves directly (Messenger, 1957). These contacts and close relationships with the Aro whom the Annang referred to as Inokon would come back to haunt the Annang severely.

The following account of the invasion of Annangland from the perspective of an Annang eyewitness would be summarized here to convey to the reader the extent of the brutality as well as what the Annang uniquely experienced. The story of the invasion below was told to Reverend William Groves of the Primitive Methodist Church, who arrived in Ikot Ekpene in 1915, a few years after the British invasion. Reverend Groves interviewed Chief Udo Akpabio of Ukana Ikot Ntuen in Ikot Ekpene and recorded the chief's recollection of the event (Groves, 1936). The chief was at the time of the interview about sixty years old and was the chief of Ukana Ikot Ntuen, one of the villages that later made what came to be known as the Ikot Ekpene Division in Annangland by the British colonialists. He was capable of telling the story as he saw it and the veracity of his story is established by Reverend Groves himself, who described the chief in his introduction as "a man held in high regard by all who had dealing with him." Groves (1936) went on to say about Chief Akpabio, "During all my years of residence in Ikot Ekpene I cannot recall any instance where his judgment was questioned" (p. 42).

## THE ASSAULT OF THE LONG JUJU SHRINE

On entering Arochukwu the British soldiers killed and captured many of the priests, as previously mentioned. Some escaped and among the escapees was a man named Ukpong Inokon who belonged to the blood brotherhood and who had extensive contacts and relationships with Annang people from Ifuho. He had married a lady from Ifuho and was actually seeking protection from his in-laws. From the name, it can be seen that the man was of Igbo origin but had enough contact with the Annang to be given an Annang name, Ukpong. After his escape, he found his way to Ifuho and was given sanctuary and protection by the village. Among the Annang, the concept of seeking protection from danger by merely running to others is very strong. *Ntumö*, as the practice is known, carried with it a legal and moral obligation for the pursuers to retreat. The practice is seen as a respect to those from whom the fugitive seeks sanctuary. It is not different from the modern practice of retreating from crossing a national boundary and seeking avenues through diplomacy to repatriate fugitives. It is the same as respecting territorial boundaries of nations, except that in the case of the Annang ethnic group, the individual is given the courtesy because of the general respect recognized as belonging to individuals and groups to which the fugitive has sought shelter. What the Annang did not know was that they were dealing with a group of individuals who did not know anything about their culture and who considered their culture barbaric and not worthy of respect. They were not aware that the world around them had changed. The force at their doorstep was no ordinary troop but soldiers who believed in the divine order and a worldview that puts the Africans in the last link of the divine order: God at the head, followed by the queen, the white race next, and others at the bottom of this link.

With this ignorance, the people at Ifuho armed themselves and the British soldiers fired the shot that would forever change Annang history. The British invasion force entered Ifuho and killed scores of people. Ukpong Inokon was also captured and hung with his head downward on top of a hill as a warning to all those who would dare challenge British authority. The soldiers returned later after his death and cut off his head. The hill where Ukpong Inokon was hung would later be abandoned by the Annang, who considered the grounds contaminated and desecrated. The land at Ifuho was taken over by the Catholic mission that eventually built a church there to Christianize the people.

The death and destruction at Ifuho along with the hanging of someone who ran to seek protection from his in-laws was something that alarmed the whole of the Annang clans. Word spread quickly throughout the land. Those who had escaped the killings at Ifuho took the stories with them to other clans along with the description of the invaders. These were men unlike the Aros that the Annang have known and fought with in the past. They looked different with the skin of albinos who were preserved as a sacrifice to the gods and nobody understood what they said. The chiefs and elders met with the warriors and planned strategies for the defense of their land. Because the invading army had a strategy of burning down houses, the men agreed that families should move into the forests and leave the villages deserted.

Like the locusts before them, the colonial army swept the land moving from Ifuho through Abiakpo Edem Idim to Ukana villages. Life was difficult and water from the spring and food replenishment could only be gotten at night when the people felt safe to venture out of their hiding places. At Ukana, the British soldiers met stiff resistance and were forced to retreat to Ikot Inyang village where they had camped days earlier at Chief Ibanga Udo Ekere's compound. The colonial army took some casualties and so could not advance. Several days passed before they had reinforcement and returned to Ukana. Again they met a stiff resistance and suffered several casualties, which only increased their resolve. Rather than retreat again, the invading soldiers fought harder and killed the head of the Ukana clan, Udo Esi Idomo. With mounting casualties on the Annang side, a decision was reached to surrender and cut their losses. The battle had taken a toll on many of the warriors. Several were dead and many were injured. Houses in the villages were torched and many people lost their yam racks. Most of all, the clan hollow drum (Ikorok) that was revered in the area and beaten on important occasions was also burned and destroyed. Surrendering to the imperial army required a face-to-face meeting, and so the warriors chose some emissaries to go and find the invading army. With a language barrier the group who was sent to meet the British army became a sitting target. They were killed and were mistaken for daredevils whose purpose was the killing of the imperial soldiers. It would take several more days before contact could again be made.

The terms for discussing the surrender included heavy fines and livestock. With these paid, the commander made known through an Efik interpreter that the soldiers were fighting in the name of a queen that now owned all the land. The commander gave his orders and prescribed what the new expectations were. From Ikot Ekpene the troop moved to Abak and what is now Ikot Abasi, Ukanafun, and Uyo. It is possible that the destruction of lives and property in Ikot Ekpene and Ukana had shown the other Annang clans about the brutality of the invading army. To this day, the Annang named Caucasians "*Mbom Épo*," meaning destroyers from the underworld, for their lack of sympathy and restraint. From Ukana the army advanced toward Abak and at Ukpom, Mr. Brooks was left to ensure there was peace while the troop moved and camped at Inen (Udo, 1983).

The establishment of control of Annangland was not fully complete and skirmishes with the invaders continued for several years afterward. In 1906, for example, Mr. Partridge, the district officer at Ikot Ekpene, and his Igbo interpreter named Dibue were almost killed by the people but for the intervention of Chief Ikang. Others were not so lucky, and in 1924, three chiefs in Ikot Okoro were publicly hung for failing to prevent their people from lynching colonial agents. It was the same story in Akon and Ikot Umo Essien, where two messengers were killed in 1908, except in Akon, the chief was not hung and British soldiers returned and killed others even though they might have been innocent and had nothing to do with the crime. The scenario was repeated in Abak in 1909 and in Abiakpo and towns in the Afaha Obong clan. The skirmishing in Afaha Obong spread to Abak and required additional British troops under Captain Duncan and later Captain Smith to put down the rebellion (Udo, 1983). The security interests of the colonial state required that troops be made available at all times to put down insurrections and rebellion in Annangland. This was perhaps the most important reason for stationing troops at Ikot Ekpene until 1933. In fact, the resistance to colonial rule in Annangland continued and reached an appalling level between 1943 and 1948 in what is known as the leopard killings (Nwaka, 1986).

The resistance of the Annang served as proof of what the Efik, the missionaries, and the European traders in Calabar told about the inhabitants of the hinterland. It was therefore important to keep some soldiers at Ikot Ekpene to deter rebellion and to keep the colonial officials safe from the people they perceived as heathens and barbarians. Thus, a small detachment was stationed at the entrance at Ikot Ekpene to check on those entering the town from Ukana and Ikpe and so was the name Control Post entered into the geography and lexicon of the town. The pacification of the Annang region by the British colonialists proved difficult and would become a source of irritation to the colonial state. What the Annang did not know was that the British had a history and a pattern for punishing groups that resisted colonialism.

## RESISTANCE

In 1904, the British invasion of the Annang region having been almost completed, the colonialists set to work. The literature is replete with the effect of colonialism in Africa; here we shall consider the after effect of the British invasion and its implications for the Annang. At the center of our analysis of the effects of colonialism lies the realization that colonialism was more than a change in political system and involved issues of identity and relationships between the Annang and the British on one hand and between the Annang and their neighbors on the other. The experience and effect of colonialism was and continues to be long-lasting for the Annang.

As Mbembe (2001) reminded us, the slave trade and colonialism echoed one another with issues that still have not disappeared. Freedom and full equality have still not been made available to the Africans, and the very definition of what it means to be human has been twisted through the manipulation of identity and classification. Kilty and Haymes (2004) further reminded us that European expansion and imperialism made racial and ethnic classification a critical issue because of the evolutionary and racist concepts of the period. The problem was that it was based on racism and imperfect knowledge of the groups to be classified by amateur ethnographers. With experience and lessons learned in India, British colonialism also required the creation of tribes and clans based on a preset taxonomic calculus (Young, 1985). Faced with a large population between the Cross River and the Niger River, the British set out to implement policies from the colonial playbook: they classified the people. As Young again observed, "The standard presumption was of discrete, bounded groups, whose distribution could be captured on an ethnic map" (1985, p. 74). Anything that suggested a similarity between groups was taken at face value, be it rites, names, or language. The language in turn was standardized forcing a common identity between two formerly different and autonomous groups, bringing forth what Young (1985) called "reformulation identities." The missionaries contributed to this process through book translations and the teaching of new languages in schools. In southeast Nigeria, the Annang, Efik, and Ibibio were lumped together as Efik through the adoption of the Efik language as the medium of instruction in 1933. Though the Ibibios protested and refused to be taught what they called "slave language," the colonial office forced all in the area to learn Efik (Noah, 1988). This eventually became a designation given to all those who lived in the area regardless of ethnicity. Thus, the Annang were called Efik up until the civil war in Nigeria in 1967. We shall return to this issue again when we examine the politics of identity in the postcolony and would see how the Annang identity has been changed and rechanged since the invasion of 1904.

The British had a habit of punishing groups who resisted colonialism through reclassification and the arrangement of new administrative structures. Besides being punitive, the need for security required that the power of bellicose groups who resisted the invasion be minimized (Young, 1985). The British learned this lesson well in Uganda between the Bunyoro and the Buganda, two rival groups. When Frederick Lugard was sent from India to Uganda to establish British colonialism there, he would learn a valuable lesson that would help to establish British dominance in Annang. Like the Annang, the Bunyoro resisted colonialism and fought to maintain their freedom; their rival the Buganda group was rewarded and expanded and in effect reducing the Bunyoro territory to a shadow of its old self. Thus as Young (1985) again reminded us, policies of the colonial state "dramatically altered the existing cultural geography" (p. 73). It was not an accident therefore that Ikot Ekpene was later transferred into what was called Uyo Division.

There was another method used in Annang known as the Ankole Pattern (Young, 1985), which the British invented in Uganda and employed throughout their colonies. In Uganda two groups, the Hima and Iru, were merged together and a new and alien name was imposed on the artificial group. The British chose to call their new creation Banyankole and imposed a new administrative unit on this group called Ankole (Segal and Doornbos, 1976). The Ankole Pattern was used in Ikot Ekpene immediately following the invasion. Part of Annangland consisting of several clans, among which were Abiakpo, Adiasim, Ikpe, Ekpenyong, Utu, Ukana, Midim, Ukanafun, and others, and were lumped together with the Ibibios from Itu, Ibiono, and Ikono and called Enyong. Thus, the Ankole Pattern was repeated and implemented in Annang. The British changed this designation when they created Annang Division. They later would merge several clans in Annangland in 1934, namely Utu, Ekpu, Ebom, Abiakpo, and Nyama, and gave the new administrative unit a name "Otoro" in what is presently Ikot Ekpene. To be fair, Britain was not the only European power in Africa who engaged in the reclassification of the people. The Belgians preferred Lingala speakers to Kikongo in the Democratic Republic of Congo, and though the former had fewer speakers, they taught Lingala and therefore forced the more numerous Kikongo speakers to learn the minority language.

The problem with this colonial policy of classification was that they knew very little or nothing about the land and the people that they were dividing into units. Mr. Luke, one of the people in the Aro expedition, later confessed to Livingstone (1916):

> What is sad about the Aro expedition is that nearly all the town names in connection with it are unknown to those of us who thought we had a passable knowledge of Old Calabar . . . it is somewhat humiliating that after over fifty years work as a mission, the district on the right bank should be so little known to us. (Livingstone, 1916, p. 192)

The colonialist knew very little about the people and cared little about issues of affiliation and ethnicity. It was a known fact that the new classifications, for reasons of convenience to the colonialist and as a punitive measure against those who resisted colonialism, ignored the cultural geography and history of the Africans. Yet the colonialists regulated the lives of those they found, and as Perham (1936) observed, the British agents regulated the lives of the Annang without knowing anything about their history and social customs.

As noted earlier, though the Annang did not have the institution of royalty as practiced elsewhere, they had chiefs and leaders whose authority was derived from tradition. Following the establishment of colonial administrative rule in Annangland, the chiefs were made servants of the colonial state. They were given caps with numbers and the British crown in the front of the cap to designate their area of origin, and no business could be conducted with agents of the colonial state if a chief did not wear his cap. Thus, the influence and authority of the chiefs were reduced. Economically, the chiefs became poorer. Udo Akpabio lamented to Reverend Groves, the Primitive Methodist Church missionary, "Things have changed very much during the last few years . . . the old men and chiefs are much poorer than the young men today" (Perham, 1936, p. 57). Other spheres of life were equally affected by colonialism for the Annang. Men were no longer allowed to use their mother's names as their last name and certain positions held by women in society were transferred to the men. Western patriarchy was introduced to the Annang in the name of civilization and Christianity. Missionaries insisted that children take their father's last name and preached that the divine order gave men more authority than women. To these Christians, taking the father's name was obedience to a divine command.

Courts were established and the chiefs as already mentioned became servants of the colonial state (Ekanem, 2002). Village and clan boundaries in Annang were no longer recognized, but individuals from different clans were sent elsewhere to settle differences, for instance in what is now Ikot Ekpene,

Okodi Iya, Akpan Etok Akpan of Ikot Esetang Uruk Uso, and Udo Akpabio of Ukana Ikot Ntuen were made warrant chiefs and sat in the same court to hear cases involving Annang from several clans who in the past took their cases to the Afe Nkuku in their own clans. Other clan heads were no longer permitted to hear cases and in effect were demoted and stripped of their positions. A charge of eighty manilas (the indigenous currency) and a fowl was required for summons and warrants, and when the colonialists discovered that it was an enormous amount for the natives, they reduced the amount to sixty manilas (Groves, 1936). The currency was later changed to the imperial unit. The Annang were also required to provide free labor to the colonial agents and carry the white agents on their heads as a form of transportation from one point to another over many miles. If the chief failed to send people to carry the white agents on time when the service was demanded, he was arrested and fined unless he could prove that he had given a particular individual a zinc disc with a number provided by the colonial office. If such proof was provided, the individual who had the disc would be arrested and fined for not reporting for work. The work was assigned to villages and it became the responsibility of the chiefs to ensure that manpower was provided. Chief Akpabio reported that because of the heavy demands of the work, men, women, and children were not exempted (Groves, 1936).

## TAXATION

If the Annang had thought that things were hard, they did not realize that things were going to get more difficult. Perhaps more than any other thing, the issue of taxation precipitated a lot of the changes and the issues of identity that would affect future generations.

In 1927 the Legislative Council in Lagos passed the Native Revenue Amendment Ordinance in the southern provinces of Nigeria, and by 1929 taxes were collected using methods invented in ancient times and perfected in India. The imposition of taxes on all in the area resulted in raising old wounds and was seen as a demonstration of the oppressive tendencies of an arrogant victorious band. Among the provision of the Revenue Ordinance, however, was one that gave each district a latitude and freedom to develop its system of assessment and tax collection (Noah, 1987). In Annang, the colonial agents gave the responsibility of assessment and collection to the heads of the extended family units (Étufök) and imposed on them the responsibility of providing roles of taxable adults to the tax office. In return for these services, the Étufök received 10 percent of all taxes collected as compensation. The rule made it mandatory and defined taxable adults as males sixteen years and older (Messenger, 1957). The taxes ranged between three and seven shillings on every taxable adult and made nonpayment a criminal offense (Noah, 1987).

The problems with this colonial tax were its severity and arbitrariness. Names of sixteen year olds provided by the Étuföks did not consider the ability to pay. Names recorded in the tax roles were seen as revenue to the colonial state and severe punishment accompanied tax debtors. To escape the punishment from the colonial state, these children that the colonial state considered taxable adults ran away from homes to other parts of the country. Such taxes were transferred to the parents when the child could not be found unless the parents were able to prove that he was dead (Groves, 1936). As can be imagined, using the Étuför this way to collect taxes brought enmity between the head of the family and other members. Because 10 percent of taxes collected belonged to the Étuför, other members accused him of disloyalty and considered him a sellout for economic gain. This lowered the respect that belonged to the Étuför position and destroyed the Annang tradition and culture. Taxation was a colonial yoke and was seen as one more reason why the colonialists should be resisted.

The resistance to colonial administration came again in 1929 in what the Annang called Éköñ Iban and was popularly called the Aba Women's Riot in Nigerian historical parlance. The disturbance began in the Ukanafun area and spread throughout Annangland. Contrary to revisionist history, the rebellion began in Annang. The story as gathered by the commission of inquiry appointed by the colonial government had it that the problem began in Oloko village in the former Owerri Province (Report, 1929). Besides the immediate causes that would be dealt with, it is important to place the Women's War in Annang in its global historical context.

Palm oil and kernel arose as the premier articles of trade following the abolition of the slave trade. The Annang as others around the Niger Delta had come to depend on the international trade in palm produce. Middlemen would buy the products in the hinterland from the Annang producers and sell it to the Europeans on the coast. Between 1914 and 1929, a period that is recognized in colonial history as the era of the consolidation of British colonial rule in Africa, giant corporations backed by the colonial state exploited African traders (Ewelukwa, 2005). Prices of the goods produced by Africans went down while the prices of European-made goods imported into Africa increased. The Annang traders saw their means of livelihood diminishing as the European traders got richer. Rules of trade changed and rechanged with alien terms that were favorable to the foreign traders. The world economic situation brought on by the British war efforts in World War I did not help.

At home, oppressive taxation laws described earlier saw young men fleeing the villages to escape arrest for not paying taxes to the colonial state. The chiefs found themselves helpless and many in the service of the colonial agents became corrupt. Work that was formerly done by men now involved women as they worked and toiled cleaning the homes and offices of colonial officers without pay. Many had been arrested, and because there were no prisons for women in the early days, female offenders, many arrested for domestic issues, were handed over to corrupt Igbo interpreters to be kept until required by the colonial courts (Groves, 1936). Many of the women suffered sexual abuses in the homes of these captors. With abuses rampant and rights curtailed, the situation in the land was a fuse that was just waiting for a spark to go off.

The colonial government provided that spark in 1929 when it decided on a census to ascertain the number of males, females, and livestock in eastern Nigeria (Report, 1929). The Annang saw the census as another way of fortifying the oppressive colonial tax system. Rumor spread rapidly that census enumerators were actually tax agents. One enumerator did not help matters when he told the people in Oloko village that the result of the census would be most likely used for tax purposes. The women took up arms and about 10,000 to 15,000 stormed administrative offices and company headquarters. They demanded, among other things, a halt in the decline in the price of palm products, a modification of the tax laws, and a review of trading rules (Ewelukwa, 2005). The riot spread quickly, and in Annangland, the men who were not done with the insurgency disguised themselves as women and joined the war. It took on a more serious tone as the Annang stormed government buildings and company stores. The Annang men quickly saw the white men as "worshipper of women," and so they believed that disguising themselves as women would draw a lesser response from the white men and so they would not be shot (Akpan, 1967). They were wrong and they soon discovered that the response was swift and brutal. More than fifty were shot and many more were arrested and detained. The insurrection was quickly put down and a commission of inquiry was set up by the colonial authority to look into the disturbances in the Calabar and Owerri provinces (Ewelukwa, 2005).

*Chapter Five*

# Western Education and the New Class

In June 1905, the inhabitants at Ikot Obong, having heard about the usefulness of Western education, requested that a school teacher be sent to their village to run a school house. The problem was that there was no teacher available, though there was a desire on the part of Mary Slessor, the Scottish missionary, to open up the area for Christian mission. The only person who could read and write was a young boy, only twelve years old, named Etim. Mary Slessor's biographer, Livingstone (1916), noted that Etim could "read English well" (p. 218). On her trip to Ikot Ekpene Ms. Slessor took the twelve-year-old boy along and left him at Ikot Obong as the new school teacher to "[form] a school and the nucleus of a congregation." The arrangement was that the village would give Etim food and the mission would pay him five shillings a month. Of this new school and the "school teacher," Ms. Slessor noted in her diary:

> I trust that it will be the first of a chain of stations stretching across the country. The old Chief is pleased. He told me that the future, the mystery of things, was too much for him, and that he would welcome the light. (Quoted in Livingstone, 1916, p. 218)

That "light" was to be spread by a mere child barely old enough to take care of himself. This story of the establishment of the school at Ikot Obong was not an isolated case. Education was a tool for evangelism and making the African Christians required every available means. Ironically, some of the young Africans cared little about the religious instruction and saw it only as an avenue to Western education. Hope Waddell (1863) told a story in his memoir about the son of Ekpo Jack. The young man had been ordered by the father to attend Reverend Waddell's school so he could learn about trade.

The young lad was surprised that instead of being taught trade, he was only taught to "saby God." Unafraid, he turned to Reverend Waddell and made clear to him that his father sent him to school "to saby trade book" and that he did not "want to saby God" (p. 289). Disappointed, the missionary used the opportunity as an evangelizing moment to teach about the immanence and omnipotence of his God. Yet education and evangelism went hand in hand for the missionary needed literate converts who could read the Christian canon and pass on the new religion. Later, Western education would be sold as a path to liberation from physical labor and a reward for civilization.

However, not everyone agreed that Western education was the path toward liberation. In fact, some saw in the new process a system that brought deceit, fraud, and evil. It demonstrated a challenge to cultural norms. Reverend Waddell himself told another story to illustrate this point in 1855. A young woman who worked as a sales clerk for King Eyo Honesty II after attending the mission school discovered that her account was deficient after sales. In order to hide her fraudulent activity she approached a young man who had attended the missionary school with her and asked that he alter the books in exchange for sex. The king later discovered this fraud and this became a great scandal. It confirmed what the critics of Western education had been saying at the time, that "everyone who handled a pen would become a forger and a cheat and a falsifier of trade papers" (Waddell, 1863, p. 569). The young woman ran away from home and left the employment of the king. The ability to read and write through the mission school was seen as capable of infecting the soul and the very nature of those who attended the schools.

Yet the mission school grew, though some were reluctant to send their children. The missionaries themselves did not help matters when they forbade their pupils from attending indigenous religious sacrifices and from participating in festivals including initiation into Ekpo secret society. Hereditary positions and functions took a great blow and parents lamented the loss of heirs to what were formally inherited offices. It was not a surprise, therefore, that certain individuals, chiefs, and religious heads, for example, kept their favorite children at home while those who were farther away in line to inherited positions were sent to the mission schools. In the words of Hardage (2002), the introduction of Western culture and education brought "great social and political upheaval" (p. 181). The school house and the church house were often located on the same property.

The education of the natives began with the establishment of orthography and the translation of simple works into the local language. The variant of the language often spoken around the mission station became the standard and official language taught in the school. Waddell wrote about his efforts to translate the St. John's Gospel into Efik. This was followed by John Bunyan's

Pilgrim Progress. The young people who could learn quickly and were able to read and write often after two years were used as teachers to teach others. As Hardage (2002) again observed, the "each-one-teach-one principle" later espoused by Frank Laubach was already employed by the missionaries in southern Nigeria before it became popular elsewhere. This method would later be employed by the Methodists who arrived in the early 1900s to establish schools first at Oron and then in Ikot Ekpene in 1905. This author's father became conscripted and sent to establish schools for the Methodists in Ikpe Ikot Akpan and Ukana Ikot Ide both in Annangland.

Those who attended the mission schools were taught about the primitiveness of their own culture. If education is the process of transmitting the cultural heritage of a people that needs to be perpetuated, what the mission schools and later the colonial schools taught the Africans were for the interest of the colonial enterprise. Rodney (1974) observed that education was an "objective necessity to keep colonialism functioning" (p. 272). The educated Annang therefore saw in the old traditions a useless society that does not correspond to the new worldview brought by the Europeans and therefore they challenged the authorities of the chiefs and violated traditional norms. The Annang society became divided. Sir Bernard Bourdillon, governor of Nigeria, noted several classes of Nigerians in a paper he presented before the Richard's Constitution publication: "the professional, salaried and trading class and the primary producers—the natives overlooked by the educated" (cited in Akpan, 1967, p. 22). The fact remains that the professional and salaried group saw the vacuum of power and trained in a foreign culture, advocated for power, and sought to take on the responsibility of the old chiefs. They were the members of what came to be known as the Ibibio Welfare Union.

## IBIBIO WELFARE UNION

Nothing has been used to justify the reclassification of Annang as the Ibibio Welfare Union (IWU; later renamed Ibibio State Union), a welfare organization arranged by the newly educated Annang and Ibibio men (they were mostly men) seeking legitimacy and a voice in the colonial administration (Nwaka, 1986). As will be demonstrated shortly, the union filled a vacuum left by the disruption of the traditional society. Values were changing fast and what was expected lacked a consensus. Let us then examine the conditions that led to the formation of the union and in the process attempt an analysis of Ikot Ekpene, where the union was formed. The history of the period would show that the union arose because certain individuals, not the entire Annang, sought to align themselves with the conditions of the time as a foil to the radical elements who advocated violence against the colonial state. The aim here is to argue that rather than use the formation of the union as evidence for the surrender of the Annang identity, the organization was formed to serve a particular purpose and was not intended to serve the reclassification exercise of the colonialist. We shall begin the examination of the etiology of IWU by first looking at Ikot Ekpene at that historical period in order to understand the need for an organization.

The history of the Ibibio Welfare Union began with Udosen Obot, who left the Primitive Methodist Mission because of frustration with Reverend Groves and James Udo Eka, who came from Uyo and served as a teacher at the Methodist School Ikot Obong Edong. The friendship between the two individuals led to the realization that an organization of educated men (only men joined the group initially) was needed in the Annang and Ibibio regions. The 1920s was a period in which many Africans elsewhere in the colonies were forming organizations to seek a voice and an audience with the colonial state.

## ETHNICITY AND THE NEW CLASS

It is important to point out here that the formation of the IWU had nothing to do with a general agreement among the Annang regarding its organization. Those who got together did not represent the society but themselves, as was shown earlier. It was a private organization that attracted a lot of people when individuals discovered its benefits. The history and function of the IWU have remained a subject of debate and speculation (Offiong, 1991; Noah, 1988). Some researchers and politicians have variously used the IWU as a referent point to advocate either assimilation of all formerly autonomous groups in southeast Nigeria or, in others, have used it to advocate separation. Noah, referring to the minutes of the union, argued:

> the minutes are a roll call of Ibibio's "Who is Who" of the time the dimension of which went much wider than the now shrunken Ibibioland to include the Annang, Oron, Enyong, Eket, Ibuno and many others some of whom no longer admit to be Ibibio. (Noah, 1988, p. 4)

Interestingly, the same argument is also used by the Igbos for the same reason, namely that of conferring Igbo ethnicity to all who live in southern Nigeria. Recent works about ethnicity in southern Nigeria tend to make claims about all in the area using historical trajectories. These arguments tend to pick a point in history as defining the ethnicity of the other and therefore conferring a right on one, usually the politically powerful group to define and claim others. Chambers (2005), for example, seizing on the fact that Igbo slaves to the new world left from the Calabar coast, sought the Igboization of all slaves in Virginia in the Antebellum period. But more than this, and for the purpose of this discussion, may be introduced the argument of Uzoigwe (2004), who argued using a European amateur ethnographer's account, that all who live between the Niger and the Calabar rivers are Igbos. He goes on to lament: "Today, some of the Igbo-speaking peoples who inhabit the periphery are literally bending over backwards to deny their Igboness" (p. 141). He is however quick to point out that though the groups in Southern Nigeria may not fit neatly into his taxonomic categories, they nonetheless could be conferred with Igboness because they constitute and benefit from what he calls the "Igbo Culture Theatre."

The confusion with the proper group identity of various groups living in southern Nigeria prior to independence evolves from various sources. As we have already seen, the colonial state and the missionaries in Africa engaged in classification exercises for different reasons. For the colonialists, some reasons were punitive and others were done for the security of the colonial state and for administrative convenience. Yet there were other reasons for the confusion that has become a legacy of the colonial enterprise. To this must be added, as already mentioned, the ignorance of amateur ethnographers who saw the African society from the evolutionary lens of the Victorian period. These "travelers" who collected stories to impress the home audience in the words of Perham (1936) saw Africa as "a field for the collection of strange customs or quaint handiwork" (p. 12). It is needless to say, therefore, that much of what was written about groups in Africa had nothing to do with how the various African groups defined themselves. James Africanus Horton, for example, wrote in the nineteenth century that the "empire of the Igbos" included the extensive and well-watered tract of territory between the River Niger and Old Calabar, and Dr. William Baikie also wrote about the Igbos as occupying between the River Niger and Old Calabar.

Why this confusion persists and has become part of the political issues in Africa and Nigeria specifically extends beyond historical reasons. The claims of ethnicity and ethnic belongingness delineating who is in and who is out, who rules and who serves have contributed to the instability of the continent today. It is not therefore an accident that those who are involved in the claims making have been the educated and elite classes who have more to gain by these claims. Representative democracy in Africa has exerted a new demand, namely that of representation in a multicultural society. The Nigerian central government, like other African governments, has glossed over the minority groups in the country and has established artificial groups, much like the colonialists did. The current state structure in Nigeria through which the oil money is shared between the central government and the states has no historical, economic, or ethnic justification. The structure relies on political arm twisting by a powerful individual or group and at other times is used to break up organized opposition. Who constitutes the citizens of a particular state relies on the claims of powerful individuals and groups. The new artificial grouping requires that individuals send a representative to the center. Who gets to pick the representative and consequently reap the benefits of participation becomes a struggle that requires a claim on the other to limit opposition. Thus, some research and work on issues of ethnicity and history among the intellectual elites in many African communities have become what Pratten (2006) described as the narrative of contested rights. As Mbembe (2001) reminded us, what passes as democracy in Africa today is nothing more than the apportionment and struggles for new rights. Those like the Annang who lack power lose the right to work, the right to individual representation at the center, and even the right to define themselves. Various administrations in Nigeria, for example, have refused to even listen to the reasons why an administrative unit (a state) through which the oil money is shared between the central government and the ethnic groups should be created for the Annang. This, therefore, for the Annang is a real-life consequence of what Greenwood (1985) refers to as regional political claims. Colonization shifted and changed the cultural geography of the region and affected the people in several ways. Let us then examine some effects of colonization in order to understand what would follow.

## EFFECTS OF COLONIZATION

The formation of unions and groups in the early decades of the last century in Nigeria was a reaction by the educated class to colonialism. The Ibibio Welfare Union, for example, like other organizations of the time, was formed as a response to colonialism. The introduction of Western culture and education by the missionaries following the colonization of southeast Nigeria was traumatic to the ethnic identity and sense of group belongingness. As stated earlier, the Annang worldview, history, and culture were arrested. What made sense and nonsense no longer followed a consensus but dictated by alien powers that saw themselves as superior to what the Annang knew as reality. The authority of the chiefs and elders understood as derived from years of tradition was declared meaningless and their position as representatives of the spirit world in the Annang cosmology became nonsensical. Instead the very position of the Akuku who made laws and whose wisdom and authority decided important dates such as planting, harvesting, and feasting were rendered ridiculous and irrelevant. The colonial agents, as already mentioned, made the Akuku servants of the colonial state. He was to wear the symbol of this low office in the form of a cap with a number and symbol of a foreign queen. To make matters worse, the Akuku, formerly seen as a symbol of authority and protection, was now given the responsibility of reporting taxable adults to the colonial authorities. This new function rendered a once revered head a symbol of reproach and hate.

With the Akuku brought low, it followed that the worldview of the Annang fell apart. It was difficult to know what to believe, what to hold on to, and what to see as fleeting. The missionaries further released trauma to the Annang; Christian cosmology condemned the belief in the ancestors and gave cherished beliefs and what sustained the society derogatory characterization. Evangelization and acculturation became one as the missionaries with their Darwinian ideas looked at the Annang as primitive. The aim of evangelization under such perspective became that of saving the Africans from themselves and rescuing them from primitivity. Rescuing the perishing and saving the dying in the old Christian hymn took on added meanings. The missionaries saw themselves as agents of divine benevolence.

Colonization affected all facets of the Annang society, including the very practice of teaching the young what it means to be human. Cultural and ethnic socializations in which parents explicitly or implicitly transmitted the history, legacy, customs, and traditions of the society were either made illegal or rendered useless in the face of racist and alien practices. The social science literature has long acknowledged the effect of the lack of ethnic socialization (Stevenson et al., 2002; Rodriguez et al., 2006). Among the Annang, this lack of transmission of what it means to be an Annang man or woman came with a devastating consequence. It meant that the moral fabric that held the society together fell apart. It meant that the authority of the ancestors as given to the Akuku, witnessed by the elders, and administered throughout the land became nothing. There was no longer any legacy to fall back on, no pride that made the people human, and no history that was worth transmitting because the missionaries told the people that they were in a great darkness and were rescued by the benevolence of the missionaries' God. Thus, the Annang tradition and culture were seen as instruments of death while the Annang were told that they who were formally in darkness have seen a great light through the benevolence of the European mission agents. Besides the religious reasons to be thankful, the colonialists and the missionaries jointly saw the Africans as children who should be taught and paid no attention to the rich African traditions. At a meeting of the Ibibio Welfare Union in 1929, for example, Reverend Groves, who served as a missionary of the Primitive Methodist Church in Ikot Ekpene, told the gathering that it is important for religious and health reasons to observe sanitary rules (Noah, 1988). Given such conditions, young men and women refused to take pride in their Annang heritage. Past penal practices either became outlawed or abandoned and the traditional society failed to be relevant in the lives of the young.

What became important was Western education, and wherever the missionaries and the colonial agent went, they preached the importance of acquiring Western education. Those who acquired such education were pointed to as liberated, and work in the civil service for these educated Africans was pointed to as a reward and the fruit of pulling oneself out of the traditional society (Mbembe, 2001). The Africans therefore were made to see traditional economic activities as primitive and as belonging to the realm of those not yet liberated through the acquisition of Western education. To be a part of the civil service and participate in its functioning were seen as the ultimate in individual achievement. To remain relevant and to secure a foot in the door in this new arrangement required education, thus Western education became much more than acquiring knowledge, it meant participation in what was seen as new, liberating, and civilized. Overnight, through the conquest of the African, what was considered valuable changed. The new values were no longer titles and membership in the warrior society but acquiring new language and strange customs. The society suffered a great trauma and what happened in Africa in the aftermath of colonialism is not different from what mental health clinicians describe as post-traumatic stress disorder (PTSD). In fact, the group trauma suffered by Africans can be described as post-colonial stress disorder (PCSD). In the present narrative, the Annang witnessed the death of relatives and important members of the community as the colonial army marched in. The fear and helplessness in the face of such overwhelming firepower can only be imagined; the community relived that experience every day, long after the canon had stopped firing.

## IKOT EKPENE AS THE CENTER OF THE STORM

We shall now turn our attention to Ikot Ekpene as a way to make sense of and understand how the Annang identity would change following the British invasion. Focusing on the town is important for a number of reasons, chief of which is the fact that the British colonialists put their focus on the town as a way to pacify the Annang, knowing full well that a town is central in the stories and culture of individuals. As was shown previously, Ikot Ekpene became a center of the colonial struggle when the people of Ifuho fought against an alien force that would not understand the simple concept of protection seeking (utumŏ agwo). But more than this mundane reason, we place Ikot Ekpene at the center of our analysis because the town would later play a prominent role in the founding of the Ibibio Welfare Union, later renamed the Ibibio State Union, an organization formed by the educated Africans for liberation, as has been pointed out. In fact, contrary to speculations in the works of some historians (Noah, 1988), the Ibibio State Union was founded in Ikot Obong Edong in Ikot Ekpene but was later moved to Uyo (Udoma, 1988). Let us begin the examination of this town by noting its underlying sociological state at the turn of the last century.

To state that Ikot Ekpene was going through what sociologists refer to as social disorganization is to recount the obvious as already noted earlier. Because of colonialism, the norm in the Annang society was no longer known and nobody knew what was expected of individuals within the society. The Annang culture had been challenged by the new colonial laws and what was considered appropriate or inappropriate rested on the assumptions of alien systems and cultural interpreters. Consensus directed by the chiefs and elders broke down and the new colonial and Western culture, though it challenged the indigenous ways, failed to produce new rules to fill the void. What resulted was therefore a society in a state of social disorganization. It is important to understand this in order to appreciate the efforts of some Annang leaders who looked for ways to make sense of their new situation.

Such was the state of the town at the beginning of the last century. The establishments of a colonial administrative post in Ikot Ekpene as a result of its strategic location and history of resisting colonialism continued to draw neighboring groups, namely the Ibibio and the Igbos. The assault from dual fronts—the colonialists and the missionaries—with new influx of Annang neighbors changed the town dramatically. We have already seen the assaults from the invasion but it is worth noting to deal with issues of morality as the town grew. With traditional oath taking outlawed by the colonial state and the missionaries mocking the people with their "foolish superstitions," the spiritual foundation was removed and individuals had nothing to fear. Punishment for wrongdoing, according to the new worldview brought by the missionaries, was only met in the afterlife. But then there was also redemption and individuals had a chance to "repent" by simply saying they were sorry and "repenting" as directed by the new religious agents. At the mundane level, one could buy one's way out of retribution by either bribing or paying a fine to the colonial state. Concepts of individual and collective punishment became blurred and followed no particular pattern. Whole villages were sometimes wiped out if European agents were harmed, as the people in Ikot Okoro in Abak and Okon in Ikot Ekpene knew firsthand when three colonial agents were killed. The colonialists could administer any kind of punitive measure whenever it suited them, including death. Yet what was seen as punishment for transgressions in the colonial penal system were mild compared to the effect of Mbiam in the Annang tradition, which the people believed was more potent. Messenger (1957) reported that the mere presence of Mbiam at a trial was enough to elicit truth. Swearing on the Bible in the colonial court, on the other hand, was seen as having no power compared to Mbiam.

In this new set up, as already mentioned, there arose a new class that could speak the new language and played a part in the administration of the new rule. The civil servants became a new class. At first they were from areas that had seen colonialism earlier and had benefited from Western education. The Yorubas and former slaves from Liberia and Sierra Leone came to work as clerks in the new civil service in Ikot Ekpene. The Igbos from Onitsha and Enugu, towns several hundred miles away, who attended missionary schools also came and worked at Ikot Ekpene as interpreters and clerks. The Efiks from the east who had attended Presbyterian mission schools in the 1800s came in large numbers also to work for the colonial state. The newly established mission schools in Ikot Ekpene recruited Efik teachers to teach Annang children. These new teachers brought with them certain behaviors that would affect the society for a long time. Because the new arrivals could speak the language of the colonial masters and interact with them, they had status and opportunity that very few of the natives did. The new arrivals understood the white colonialists and served as interpreters. Thus, they had power and influence over the indigenous people. They became symbols of opportunities and possibilities in the new society. They embodied what a native could become if he or she plays by the new rules and give up resisting colonialism. With their bicycles, long stockings, and well-ironed shorts, they exuded affluence and influence, having moved away from primitive vocations such as farming into new exalted and cleaner positions as clerks and civil servants. They had houseboys and housegirls, fellow Africans like them who were little more than slaves and who did their every bidding. They dress and spoke differently; indeed they were the faces of the new rule. They became colonial agents in their own right and reenforced the messages of the missionaries who educated them. Yet they were not equal with the white men despite efforts to be players in the new administration; these African civil servants were still seen as outsiders by their masters who did not trust them. It was not a surprise, therefore, that by 1933 the colonialists dismissed all Liberians and Sierra Leoneans from the colonial civil service in Nigeria (Fafunwa, 1974). Something needed to be done to get into the good books of the masters by this new indigenous elite. Shut out by the colonialists and disallowed from serious participation in the colonial political process, the educated indigenous elite devised a method. Rather than fight against the colonial state, they found ways to work within the system by aligning themselves with their white rulers. They saw the new system as a better way and organized themselves as the new converts and disciples of the civilization enterprise. They could not return to the old ways and the new way was shutting them out. This is how the Ibibio Welfare Union had its beginnings, and in the next chapter we will look at this organization and the part it played in the history of colonialism in southeast Nigeria.

In this chapter we have explored the beginnings of education and its effects in the early colonization of the Annang. We have also looked at the role of the educated Africans. We have described colonization as a group trauma and its accompanying stress. Colonialism and the attitude of the missionaries showed the civil service as a reward of participation in the civilization enterprise. Tribal groups were set to compete with each other, and those who acquired Western education gained advantage over those who did not. The practice and process of seeking domination of the smaller groups by the larger ones in Nigeria had its origin in this period.

## Chapter Six

# Confronting Change

Much has been written about the Ibibio Welfare Union (IWU) and Annang and Ibibio nationalism that began as a response to colonialism in Nigeria (Offiong, 1991; Udomah, 1991; Noah, 1987a, 1987b). Those who joined the organization sought relevance and a place at the colonial policy table through participation in the organization. The organization was a means to an end and was not demonstrative as an end in itself. As noted earlier, the social disorganization occasioned by the introduction of an alien system could hardly be the stuff through which individuals defined themselves, but as drowning people, the Annang, as we shall see, clutched onto whatever straw was available. It is important to keep in mind that those who formed the Ibibio Welfare Union were private individuals who joined a private organization without consulting the Annang elders who had been made irrelevant and obsolete within the British colonial system, as noted in the preceding chapter.

This chapter will address the historical experiences at the time of the formation of the Ibibio Welfare Union and shall trace the development of the social conditions that led to the formation of this philanthropic and self-help organization that became a political pressure group. The chapter will further examine issues of the destabilization of the Annang society. The aim is to allow the reader to establish whether IWU was a child of necessity or an example of hegemony. As Kolapo (2004) reminded us, sociohistorical processes hardly occur singularly but are related to historical developments in other areas. Failure to recognize this phenomenon, he warns, means missing the larger historical elements that can serve as a background that illumines the historical processes. We seek to argue here that the location and logic of contemporary discourse regarding the welfare organization gloss over important historical elements.

The mobilization of young people in Nigeria for civic responsibility and disorder has been noted in the literature (Gore and Pratten, 2003), but what has not been analyzed is its historical genesis. Returning to our subject, ethnic unions were products of circumstance, for as Noah (1987b) observed, they were "practical responses to colonial situations characterized by their irritating and obnoxious demands" (p. 38). What has been characterized as ethnic unions in the early part of the twentieth century, however, were not ethnic in the true sense of the word but hastily organized groups drawn together as a response to the difficult colonial demands. Young (1985) pointed out that such territorial referents as a response to colonialism were ill defined. The organizers had no national goals of liberation except to bind together to demand freedom from colonial oppression. It is also important to point out here that it was in the interest of the colonial state to deal with discrete and smaller units as a way to foil African nationalism and frustrate vast territorial regrouping. The British, for example, discouraged Sudanese nationalism away from Unity of the Nile Valley (Young, 1985). The Africans in Nigeria especially took advantage of these preferences and launched what is sometimes described erroneously as ethnic and semi-ethnic unions. Among these unions was the Owerri Improvement Union that was launched in Port Harcourt in 1916. It was followed by the Yorubas who launched the Egba Society in 1918. Two years later, the Igbos launched another union called the Onitsha Improvement Union in Lagos in 1920. Those Ibibios who lived and worked at Calabar had what they called the Ibibio Mainland Association. It was followed by the Calabar National League (Noah, 1987b). Thus, the Ibibio Welfare Union was founded at a time when binding together to fight the colonial power was done by many groups. We cannot leave this section without mentioning that to this list of "ethnic" unions formed in the early part of the last century may be added the Ikot Ekpene Society. This, like other organizations of the period, consisted of those who acquired colonial education and who saw the formation of a union as a way to band together in the colonial state. Unfortunately, no document of the Ikot Ekpene Society is known to have survived the destruction of Ikot Ekpene during the Nigerian civil war, and most of the members of that society were killed off in that war. What has survived are some of the documents of the Ibibio Welfare Union that were in the custody of Chief Nyong Essien (Noah, 1987b).

## HISTORY OF THE IBIBIO WELFARE UNION

The Ibibio Welfare Union was the brainchild of James Udo Eka, who served as a school teacher at Ikot Obong Edong under the Primitive Methodist mission in Ikot Ekpene. He came from Uyo and moved to Ikot Ekpene like all those attracted to the colonial and mission service. At Ikot Ekpene he met Udosen Obot, another teacher who was an indigene also under the service of the Primitive Methodist Church where Reverend William Groves was the church and school superintendent and S. U. Etuk was a clerk for the colonial administrator. Udosen Obot later fell out with Reverend Groves, the British missionary, and led a push to establish an African Independent Church during the Spirit Movement. It was to this man that James Udo Eka turned with the idea of a union that would allow them to gain the trust of the colonialists and improve the welfare of the participants. A date was fixed for the inaugural meeting at the Qua Iboe Mission School at Uyo on Saturday, April 28, 1928, at 2:30 in the afternoon. No reason is given for the change in venue from the initial proposed site at Ikot Obong Edong on April 17, 1928, to a meeting at Uyo two weeks later, except that the trip to Uyo by the Ikot Ekpene participants required a tremendous effort in the days before many cars were on the road and in which the twenty-mile journey required many hours of bicycling.

On the day of inauguration, the folks from Ikot Ekpene, according to the minutes book, arrived at Uyo late after the meeting had commenced and after the initial officers were already elected. Thus, important decisions were taken at that crucial meeting without their consent and without their votes. Only two individuals from Abak, W. U. Nsasak and W. O. Ekanem, were present, and neither was appointed an officer of the new organization. When the folks from Ikot Ekpene finally arrived, they inquired about the purpose of the gathering and were presented with the aims and goals of the new organization. Thus, neither Mr. Udosen Obot nor James Udo Eka fully explained the purpose of the organization to those from Ikot Ekpene before they undertook the long trip. However, once at Uyo the following goals were given as a response to their inquiry about the purpose of the new organization:

The name of the organization was to be the Ibibio Welfare Union.
Its aim was to create unity between the people of Annang and Ibibio.
To foster the spirit of brotherhood feeling among its members.
To unite in one effort to elevate the position of the race in industry and learning.
To encourage education in every respect.
To preserve the honor of the tribe by leading law-abiding lives.
To meet from time to time to discuss matters of vital importance.
To consider the improvement of customs and manners of our people.
To try in words and actions to be patterns to the rest of the people.
To create the feelings of love and honor for whatsoever is beautiful and noble.
To prompt occasions for the congratulation and heartfelt appreciation of any uncommon achievement or success on the part of its members or its people.

To sympathize with those afflicted and those who are despised for upholding the honor and the name of Ibibio or Annang.
To try all that is possible to divert the contempt that is too frequently poured on some of the unlucky members of our race by some other tribes.
To be loyal to the country, to one another and to the British Empire
To Champion the race in general and to every good cause. (Noah, 1988, p. 74)

Two things are worthy of note in the manifest goals enumerated here, namely the vagueness and the activist nature of the goals. The aims of the organization sounded like they came from the pulpit and had everything within them that would have appealed to Christians newly converted to the faith. It made any objection as to the need for the existence of such organization as proposed nonsensical. Such framing and loftiness of the goals of the new association were not accidental. The goals were written by individuals who were affiliated with and worked for the Methodist mission and who were familiar with the basic tenets of Methodism. Thus, the issues important in Methodism and Wesleyan theology flavored the language of the organization in its early stage. The basic teaching of Methodism, that social action is an outcome of Christian belief, found its way into the minds of these early employees of the church in Nigeria. We shall return to the place of religion in the Ibibio Welfare Union, but for now let us examine further its goals and objectives as presented on that first meeting.

It is very interesting that the aims and goals as explained to the latecomers from Ikot Ekpene included unity between the two groups—Ibibio and Annang. They understood membership in the new organization as a means to enhance their position and struggle against colonialism. Both the Annang and the Ibibios were forced in late into the Nigerian union, whereas such groups as the Efiks and Yorubas had already acquired Western education and became interpreters for the colonial agents. Because British colonialism employed the indigenes as agents of the colonial state, Efik, Igbo, and Yoruba interpreters were abundant in the Annang and Ibibio areas and spoke condescendingly about the inhabitants of the area. The British colonialists saw them as primitive, and educated Nigerian sidekicks joined in and had no regard for the natives. Livingstone (1916) described those living outside of the Calabar area as weak, ignorant, and primitive. It was in the best interest of the Annang to bind together with their Ibibio neighbors to fight what they perceived as a common enemy. It is not surprising, therefore, that all those present at that meeting saw the need for an organization such as proposed by Mr. James Udo Eka, especially because he was well known in the Ikot Ekpene area and held in high regard as a school teacher. But before we go any further, it is important to return to the name of the organization as proposed in 1928.

The organization was purely a social organization from the reading of the stated goals. In keeping with their Methodist conviction of a social action being the requirement of the Christian faith, as already stated, the conveners stressed unity of individuals and groups, education, submission to authority and the law, individual behavior as an expression of learning, the need to lead exemplary lives, the appreciation of aesthetics and beauty, sympathy and compassion to those who suffer, freedom, and doing good. It was to be a welfare union with a philanthropic goal, and such a plan appealed to those who were present. They were individuals who were not necessarily indigenes of Annang because the minute book listed their places of abode and not necessarily where the individuals were born. Thus, James Udo Eka was listed as coming from Ikot Ekpene even though he hailed from Uyo. Others, like Batta who was listed as "director," was not an Annang indigene, confirming what had earlier been mentioned that ethnic unions at the beginning of the last century in the British colonies lacked specific geographic referent (Young, 1987). Another important point to mention here is that these individuals who elected to become members of the union were self-selected by education and age. It may be called elitist for they absorbed Western education and looked down on their own indigenous culture. Emboldened by the evolutionary perspectives and enlightenment theories of the Victorian curriculum as taught by the missionaries, these school graduates and semi-graduates saw themselves as beneficiaries of new knowledge and the products of the civilization enterprise. They rejected the old ways as primitive and uncivilized and saw the new European culture as the authentic path to development. Nwaka (1986) noted that "most of the members, especially the leaders, of the union were educated Christians who had acquired Christian values and prejudices about some local beliefs and practices" (p. 432). He goes on to report that during the leopard killings in southern Annang, the Ibibio Welfare Union in its report described the local people as "savageous" and "dwarfish thinkers and ridiculed . . . revered traditional institutions" (p. 432). It was not a surprise, therefore, that one of the aims of the organization was stated as the improvement of the customs and manners of their own people. Food served at the meetings further illustrates the membership of the union. In many of the meetings, as the minutes book indicates, beer and cigarettes were served. These were not indigenous, and early in the twentieth century most of our people had not yet developed a taste for these European items and cuisines, but those who were acculturated or lived in urban areas had developed what they saw as the European ways.

The position of the union was deliberately ambiguous. The union had endeared itself to the colonialists and saw itself as an ally in the civilization enterprise while seeking some power from the colonialists. This led to many expatriates and missionaries expressing an interest in becoming members of the association. In effect, the organization was not truly an ethnic organization because some expatriates became members. When the Annang women and men joined the tax riots of 1929, the Ibibio Welfare Union quickly served as a pacifying agent for the colonialists and issued a letter to many districts scolding the participants in the riots and their agents (Noah, 1988).

The letter went on to admonish the women "to remain in peace." It further advised the women that

> The members of the Ibibio Welfare Union are your true friends, brothers and well-wishers. If you wish to ask the government any question or have something to say, simply send your friendly representative to see the D.O. of your district. (Noah, 1988, p. 228)

Such a letter as this from "the union" coming as it did in the height of what was a big problem for the colonialists endeared the Ibibio Welfare Union to the colonialists and gave the leaders of the union a special place in the hearts and minds of the Europeans, while those who opposed the colonialists had no use for members of the organization.

One could readily see why these young individuals who self-selected for membership in the organization would not consult traditional leaders and elders in Annangland who were not educated and were not Christians. From the foregoing, it is safe to infer that they held the illiterate and traditional society in very low esteem, as Nwaka (1986) already pointed out. But why would the consultation be necessary? These were private individuals who voluntarily joined a private philanthropic organization.

Noah (1988) opined that the IWU member list read like a list of Who's Who in Annangland, thereby implying that those who chose not to become members in this organization were therefore not important. A list of membership of the organization says otherwise. Those who traveled from Ikot Ekpene to Uyo for the meeting of the organization were very few. In fact, at the second meeting of the organization on June 2, 1928, nobody attended the organization's meeting from Abak. Several factors contributed to this poor attendance from Ikot Ekpene and Abak, the two important Annang towns of the period. The first factor is related to the time of the meeting. At a time when transportation across the area was difficult because of the scarcity of the means of transport, having these teachers and civil servants to travel to Uyo at 2:00 in the afternoon was difficult. The Annang members themselves raised this as an issue at the second meeting of the organization at Uyo when they argued against monthly dues. Their position was that it was unfair to require monthly dues because they had to bear the cost of transportation to the meeting each month. Related to this is also the time of the meeting, which was held from 2:00 to 4:00 in the afternoon. The return trip from Uyo might have been an inconvenience because it had to have been after nightfall.

Another factor that contributed to the poor attendance from Annangland was the method of announcing subsequent meetings. No circular was issued announcing future meetings and the work of spreading notices about the organization's future meetings was left to those who attended the previous ones. Though no reason is given for opting for the latter method, it can be argued that the method might have encouraged attendance, but whether this was the actual case is in doubt.

We cannot conclude this section without mentioning an important point associated with the early days of the organization. The question of having committees to address important issues in the organization led to a decision to have representatives to form committees for each of the three centers of Abak, Ikot Ekpene, and Uyo. On July 7, 1928, at the third meeting of the Ibibio Welfare Union at Uyo, two Annang members who were present at the meeting, Mr. Ekanem from Abak and S. U. Etuk from Ikot Ekpene, opposed the formation of a nonrepresentative committee. The motion to appoint a leadership committee from the floor met with opposition from these members. They suggested that rather than appoint members from the floor, each "section" or "district" "should send its own representative who will form the committee" (Minutes, 1928, p. 79). The house voted and instructed each district to appoint its own representative to be presented to the house at the next meeting. Thus, three centers were delineated and members appointed and presented at the next meeting. The following individuals were selected to represent the three "centers" of Abak, Ikot Ekpene, and Uyo.

Mr. W. O. Ekanem was the sole representative of Abak; U. E. Obot, J. U. Udo, S. U. Etuk, T. Udo, and E. I. A. Essen represented Ikot Ekpene; and U. A. Equere, D. S. Usanga, M. D. Anana, J. B. Okokon, and J. U Utuk represented Uyo. It is worth noting that while the minutes did not mention the clans of those from Abak and Ikot Ekpene, it took the time to show the origins of the representatives from Uyo. Thus, Equere represented Ikot Ekan, Usanga was for Etinan, Anana was for Uruan, and Okokon was for Offot/Uyo (Noah, 1988).

It is important and instructive that the issue of a representative committee with semi-autonomy and separate meeting places came up so early in the life of the young organization. Rather than be seen as a symbol of hegemony, the organization actually raised old ethnic cleavages and distrusts. The individuals from the Annang area were bent on having control over who speaks for them and to ensure that their interests were represented. Among the Ibibios, the minute book showed that individuals were not chosen at random but represented Ibibio clans. It is not therefore correct as some have maintained that the early organization was an example of the acknowledgment of hegemony and nonrecognition of separate ethnic identity by the Annangs. Again, instead of the IWU being seen as an example of the sacrifice of the Annang identity, it must be seen as a social organization whose members were keenly aware of their identity and who worked to promote such identity within the same organization.

## CONTEMPORARY REALITIES

We shall now turn our attention to the examination of the political conditions that led to the formation of the Ibibio Welfare Union. The tendency to romanticize the past and make heroes of the principal characters is a known fact in the history of groups and communities. The story of the Ibibio Welfare Union is not different in this regard. In the process of retelling the idealized past, certain fallacies are committed. Yet there were certain conditions that contributed to the birth and growth of the organization. We shall deal with these conditions under the following headings, namely political, social, religious/spiritual, and lastly psychological. It is in these multifaceted lenses that the true conditions of the society would be understood. We begin here first with the political conditions.

## POLITICAL CONDITIONS

The struggle for linguistic dominance between the Efiks and the Ibibios has always been a source of contention between the two groups. Though history locates the Efiks as migrants from the Ibibio mainland to the cross-river coast, the Efiks have always prided themselves as having a superior form of the language and have displayed this linguistic chauvinism to the discomfiture of their Ibibio cousins. In 1848, with the arrival of the Presbyterian missionaries from Scotland, the Efik language, a variant of the Ibibio language, was committed to a written form by translating religious works into the language, as already noted. Thus, Bunyan's Pilgrim Progress, St. Johns' Gospel, and the Psalms became staple reading materials in the homes of Efik chiefs. Their children attended schools taught by the missionaries and their agents and read the Bible in their language. When the church spread westward into the hinterland, the Efik dialect of the language was carried along and taught to the Ibibios and the Annang. As is always the case elsewhere in Africa and among other conquered people, any language that is made a medium of instruction in the school automatically carries a prestige and becomes the language of the educated class. Efik achieved this important status.

By the early 1920s, the Phelph Stokes Commission of New York in its scathing report on British colonialism in Africa blamed the British for leaving the education of the natives chiefly to the missionaries and recommended the involvement of the imperial power in the education of the natives (Fafunwa, 1974). In an attempt to implement this recommendation, the colonial authorities called for indigenous languages to be recommended as the medium of instructions in the southern provinces of Nigeria. In the Calabar provinces, because of the memoranda submitted along with materials and work already done by the missionaries, Efik was selected by the colonial office as a medium of instruction to the great discomfiture of the Ibibios. The Ibibios saw that as the missionaries and colonial agents taking sides in an old struggle and they protested what they saw as a slight on their dignity. The matter would have been forgotten and blamed on the Ibibios' lack of power except for the sloppy handling and leaked memorandum by the Presbyterian authorities.

E. N. Amaku, an Efik man, then a headmaster of a Presbyterian school, had written a memo in support of Efik in the school to his superiors in the Presbyterian mission meant to be sent to the colonial education office. In the memorandum, Mr. Amaku gave a distorted history of the Ibibios, according to some accounts. He wrote that the Ibibios had always been Efik slaves and were known to be dishonest and untrustworthy. The memorandum was leaked to the public and uproar erupted. Many Ibibio people demanded an apology, and when Mr. Amaku escaped lynching he went into hiding. An organization known as the Ibibio Mainland Association was formed and Mr. Amaku was taken to court. Though the case was later settled out of court, Mr. Amaku was asked to pay court costs and the Ibibios obtained assurances that the wrong information would not find its way into the school curriculum or the report of the commission (Noah, 1988). What Mr. Amaku wrote, however, was a stereotype that the missionaries and colonial agents held and had long known about those who lived outside of the coast in the hinterland. The missionaries and colonial agents had long thought of those outside of Calabar as uncivilized savages. Writing about the natives in the hinterland, for example, Livingstone (1916), who wrote a biography of Mary Slessor, said, "they were one of the poorest races in Africa." He described those outside of the coast as "cowed" and "sullen," "untruthful and filthy" (p. 192). Mary Slessor, the Scottish missionary who later became a colonial agent, also seemed to have harbored prejudices against the Ibibios and Annang for on hearing that Mr. Partridge, her friend, was assigned to work among them, she wrote these words of advice to him:

> I do trust you will enjoy your work among the Ibibios. If you can discriminate between fear and stubbornness, you have won half the battle If you try to put yourself into these ignorant, besotted, cowardly Ibibios shoes, You will see how much more likely they are to fear you than to give themselves over at once. Have patience. They are deceitful as a race. (Letter to Mr. Partridge, January 6, 1905)

Perhaps Amaku was simply trying to gain acceptance, according to Noah (1988), by repeating the familiar stereotypes and ignorance held by the Europeans. Whatever his motives were, it resulted in litigation and bad blood among the Efiks, Amaku, and the Ibibios that has not fully been resolved to this day as the language controversy in Akwa Ibom State has demonstrated. Following the creation of Akwa Ibom State, the new state adopted Ibibio as a language of instruction in schools despite the fact that Efik has a long history of being taught in schools and already had a long-established literature.

The solidarity and energy from the Amaku's case emboldened many Ibibios and Annangs and opened to them the possibilities and potentials inherent in the formation of a permanent union and allowed them a glimpse into the benefits of the future. Besides ethnic politics, some saw the formation of a union as a forum to network and access whatever opportunities were available in the colonial administration. As mentioned earlier, very few opportunities were opened to the indigenes of the area in the colonial administration and whatever was available tended to be at the lower level. Thus, the natives were more likely to be cleaners, gardeners, cooks, and stewards. Those who could read and write served as low-level clerks for the missions and the colonial civil service. The formation of the union allowed those with access to share knowledge and network with those without access.

But more than this, the era can be characterized as one of agitation for meaning making. Rumbles of realignment on the part of the colonial power and the futility of disjointed struggles at the indigenous level saw very little success. Though some have seen the Ibibio Welfare Union as a symbol of ethnic hegemony, the fact remains that it was the British colonial authorities that first forced several ethnic groups into one political union. After the British established themselves in Ikot Ekpene in January 1904, they sent out an expedition to explore the neighboring Annang and Ibibio areas (Messenger, 1957). The expedition landed at Itu and then from there went to Uyo, Abak, and what was then Opobo, now Ikot Abasi. On the return of the expedition the following year, the areas were all grouped together under one control and known as Enyong District with an administrative headquarter at Itu (Messenger, 1957). With this single stroke of the pen, the British colonial authorities formally opened a new chapter in group relationships and redrew the political geography in what is now Akwa Ibom State. The Ibibio group in Opobo, along with the Annang in that area, was forced into union with the Ibibio of Itu, Uyo, Ikono, and Ibiono, groups who had before then had no contact beyond marriages and trade. It is important to note that prior to this event brought by the colonial authorities, there was no central authority that controlled the Annang and the Ibibio.

This new political structure established by the British did not last, but its importance was noted. In 1914, nine years after it was constituted, the Enyong District was broken into two districts. While the upper cross-river region remained Enyong District, Ikot Ekpene, Uyo, and Abak were lumped together as Ikot Ekpene District with headquarters at Ikot Ekpene. This new arrangement in 1914 meant that Uyo with its smaller population as compared to such dense areas as Adiasim made the Ibibios a minority in the new political structure compared to the Annang. It is therefore important to see that the formation of the Ibibio Welfare Union occurred before 1934 when Uyo became a separate district. The union, with its meetings at Uyo, allowed the members to draft rules of participation and brought the educated Ibibio and Annang who had a part to play in the new colonial civil service and education together.

Among the most disruptive part of the new arrangements was the court system. The new structure did away with native authority and food taboos and required separate groups to give up their autonomy, practices, and systems of justice for new ones. Thus, those forced together found themselves as conquered people. What was considered justice in the old system was abandoned and new rules and appeal to new authorities became the norm. The people feared the anger of their neglected gods but continued to pay homage and take instructions from others who were once seen as distant neighbors. Ibibio from Uyo had to see the district commissioner at Ikot Ekpene and an old rivalry between Annang and Ibibio was settled overnight without a shot. In the words of Nair (1972), Ikot Ekpene became the administrative and cultural capital of the Annang and Ibibio. As Messenger (1957) puts it, what the Europeans called justice reflected "the strong influence of British concepts of justice" (p. 210) and Christian ethics, so that what was once criminal became an acceptable practice overnight.

The Ibibio Welfare Union came at a time when the social, cultural, and administrative landscape was slowly being redrawn by the colonial government. With the language controversy occasioned by the E. N. Amaku memorandum and the preference of Efik dialect by the missionaries, the historical claim of the Ibibios was challenged. No longer were the Efiks seen as a group who defied the Ibibio rule; they were now the rulers and had claims to superiority, thanks to the missionaries and the colonialists. The Efik were now school teachers, preachers, and interpreters. Some had attended the mission schools and came west along with the missionaries. Those who came west looked down on the Ibibio and saw them as primitive. The seeming attention given to the Annang and Ikot Ekpene in 1914 by the colonialists and the Methodist missionaries made the need to have an umbrella organization urgent. The formation of the Ikot Ekpene Club that admitted Igbos, Efik, and all who cared to join and could afford the membership fee was another example of the educated class trying to exert its influence. Yet no new organization that would claim to speak for the Annang and Ibibio could be formed without the full participation of the Annang. Mr. James Udo Eka found an ally in Mr. Udosen Obot because both had been a part of the Primitive Methodist mission in Ikot Ekpene.

## SOCIAL AND RELIGIOUS REALITIES OF THE TIME

As Messenger (1957) again observed, the effect of these alignments and realignments through political acculturation was the destruction of whatever limited measure of political cohesiveness existed among the Annang. What he failed to note is that these realignments and new structures adversely affected and destroyed the social cohesion of both the Annang and Ibibio institutions, as already noted. No longer were individuals concerned about the importance and linkages of Iman; instead the new generation was juggling for positions within the limited sphere of colonial administration. The new realities required forced linkages and accommodation across ethnic and traditional boundaries. The Ntinya and Akuku were reduced and seen as relics of the past and the primitive. Their authorities no longer relevant, these old leaders retreated to their little huts and were seldom consulted in important matters. The Ibibio Welfare Union arose to fill that void made available by the shock and jog of colonialism. The colonial administrators banned courts that were not recognized by the colonial system. The Akuku could no longer perform one of the important functions of his office, namely that of crowning village heads, because the colonial administrators decided who was a chief and who was not. The magisterial powers of the Ntinya were abolished and his duties reduced to serving as a priest of the local shrine (Messenger, 1957). And because such office required functions proscribed by the missionaries, the Ntinya did not convert to Christianity and therefore became an outcast in a community in which many had converted to Christianity. The Iman was abolished and the people were given new identities as belonging to a unit prescribed by the colonial authorities. Thus, they saw themselves as from Ikot Ekpene Division, Uyo Division, Abak Division, and so on. Even within the same division, the people were further split into districts that crossed several

Imans, making the ancient food taboos that were identifiers impossible. This assault was completed with the missionaries telling their new converts about the folly of keeping ancient and primitive taboos in the face of the converts' newfound "freedom" conveyed by the missionaries' God. With the blending and the permeable and disappearing boundaries, it was easier to form a new organization that made claims to the commonality of those whose world had been turned upside down.

To the list of fertile conditions that led to the formation of the IWU may be added the religious and spiritual conditions of the time in Ikot Ekpene, where the idea of an organization such as the IWU emanated. As noted earlier, the two individuals, James Udo Eka and Udosen Obot, associated with the IWU, both worked for the Primitive Methodist mission in Ikot Ekpene and both were perhaps affected by the dynamics of the rapidly changing culture, political conditions, and the impermanence of what were formerly taken as given in the society. What gave life meaning was slowly going away and the individual's sense of community and citizenship was gone. What were considered materials of the assumptive and authentic world were now seen as mere superstitions that hindered human progress rather than enhance it, and so a movement arose to get rid of these false gods. Ironically, the missionaries' God failed to fill the vacuum left in the Annang worldview, and so a syncretic movement arose and like wildfire swept across the land.

## THE RISE OF THE SPIRIT MOVEMENT

Messenger (1957) gave a brief history of the Spirit Movement, as it was called, and suggested that it originated from disaffected members of the Catholic and Kwa Iboe mission, an English interdenominational missionary church. The movement began among the Igbos, Ijaw, and Andoni people who lived closer to the coast and had more extensive contact with the Christian missionaries than the Annang. No matter its origins, the movement fitted the Annang worldview and allowed the new Christian religion to be understood and practiced in familiar terms. Just as the Cubans and former slaves in the Caribbean islands turned the Christian theology to suit their worldview in the practice of Santeria, the Africans in southern Nigeria did the same but in a different way when they syncretized the missionaries' religion.

Returning to the Spirit Movement in Ikot Ekpene and its influence in the formation of the Ibibio Welfare Union, it is important to trace the missionary activities in the town as a way to understand the influence of the Spirit Movement that would follow. The first Christian missionaries arrived in Ikot Ekpene in 1919 with the arrival of the Methodist missionaries, ten years before the formation of the IWU. The Primitive Methodist Church missionaries were soon followed by the Roman Catholic Irish missionaries. According to Messenger (1957), these early missionaries, like the colonialists before them, encountered a lot of resistance from the local people, and the number of converts was really small. With an incoherent theology of a God who had a son without a wife but later wanted the only son dead to appease himself so he could save humanity, it is not difficult to see why the Annang who had endured the brutality of the war that invaded their land avoided the assembly of the white missionaries who they saw as an ally in the colonial enterprise.

Though Meek (1937) maintained that the Spirit Movement began in 1930, Jones (1989) reported that in 1927, when he was serving as the acting assistant district officer in Ikot Ekpene, the movement was in full force and those adherents of the movement were standing trial before District Officer M. D. W. Jeffreys, who the Ibibio nicknamed "Ntokon" (pepper) for his no-nonsense approach in dealing with the natives. The Spirit Movement essentially gave the European God and the Trinity characteristics of African deities and substituted the anthropomorphism of the European God and what was divine with what was known about the world. Thus, the nature of the Christian Holy Spirit known as *Alulu Nchana Nchana Chibilip* or Edisana Spirit in Efik was at the heart of the movement. Unlike the Christian Trinity, the Holy Spirit was divorced from the Trinity and given prominence above the Father and the Son much like the chief. The Son had very little influence in this theology. In this capacity, the deity was capable of curing all kinds of illness, ensuring wealth and longevity. It was also believed to have power over all other native deities and magic and was capable of destroying charms and picking out witches. In this theology, Satan was considered a deity (Nnem) who was expelled from heaven and now lives in the thick forest where he rules over lesser spirits, ghosts, and witches. Those practicing the traditional religion were helping Satan and so those in the Spirit Movement were agents of change helping the Holy Spirit fight the bad ones here on earth.

In this understanding, the Father of the trinity was syncretized as the Awachi Anyong (Supreme Deity) of the local religion. He was said to inhabit the cross on the altar, thereby turning the house of worship into a shrine where adherents could go and offer prayers and sacrifices like the local religion (Messenger, 1957). Because the spirit of the departed in the old religion could possess the wearer of the mask of the Ekpo members in the ancestor society, the Holy Spirit was also believed to possess the communicant. In the trance-like state when possessed by the Holy Spirit, just as in the old religion, those possessed could speak in strange tongues and do supernatural things. They, like those who belonged to the Idiong divinity cult of old, could see the future and enter into forbidden places without suffering the consequences of violating the sacred rules. Thus, they entered into shrines and caused a lot disturbance in the society. Possession was induced by the leaders of the movement and true believers were known to receive the Holy Spirit, demonstrated in such acts as shaking of limbs, climbing trees and roof tops, running around in the village, and rolling on the floor. Jones (1989) reported that the adherents under the influence of the spirit, who were committed to prison by Dr. Jeffreys, the district officer, "sang very loudly and danced." He added that "nobody in the station or the surrounding township was able to get any sleep, for the disturbance went on all night." The colonialists knew they had a problem in their hands for as Jones (1989) again reported, the spiritualists in the villages were "completely out of hand and were rushing about attacking, assaulting, tying up and otherwise maltreating those whom the spirit identified as witches." Though the missionaries tried to stop this menace, it was hard to tame it as it spread from village to village.

The Spirit Movement, rather than help the Annang society, joined the colonialists and the missionaries in destroying whatever was left of the Annang culture and religion. The adherents, like the missionaries, maintained that the Annang religion was a part of Satan's kingdom and that salvation was through renouncing old ways and accepting the power of the Holy Spirit. Messenger (1957) attributed the abolition of indigenous cults and shrines to the activities of the Spirit Movement. Many shrines of the indigenous religion were burned, and in many cases, the new African spiritual churches were constructed with wood from old shrines, demonstrating to the local people the power of the Holy Spirit.

Messenger (1957) opined that "the movement gained its main support from middle aged men who had some political influence but were not religious specialists" (p. 250). Open conflict was also very common between the older traditional people in the Annang society and the younger and middle-aged people who were either active participants or those who sponsored the movement and remained passive supporters. The leaders of the movement, according to Messenger (1957), were "self-appointed evangelists who could arouse the people to a high pitch of emotional fervor" (p. 252). Among those who were part of the movement were Udoesen Obot and Udo Udo Akpan Okpofut. The former would later play a big role in the establishment of the Ibibio Welfare Union and also served as its president. Very little has been written on the Sprit Movement and the people who were practitioners, which later became Ufök Akam or "houses of prayer," but for our purposes and within the limits of this discussion, it is important to point out how that social and religious experience affected those who lived through it and eventually led to the formation of what has come to be called ethnic union. The young and the middle aged who were part of the movement, according to Messenger

(1957), did not have a "lifetime of religious acculturation, which eventually would have engendered an attitude of religious conservatism" and therefore had no interest in protecting the Annang religion and culture. They saw the new religion and its variants as evidence of the efficacy of a new deity and incorporated the theology into an African worldview. It became possible to change their thinking and reach out across ethnic cleavages to others in an effort to create what they saw as a new society. This was why Udoesen Obot teamed up with James Udo Eka to create the IWU.

The missionaries responded to the Spiritual Movement by excommunicating members who got involved in it. Excommunication carried a serious consequence for it effectively cut off the excommunicants from the material benefits provided by the missionaries. Deprivation of such benefits as schools and hospitals carried real-life consequences for those that Messenger (1957) referred to as "rice Christians," those who only joined the missionaries for the material benefits. Whether they were strict adherents of the faith or not, they saw the establishment of a welfare association and its potential as helping to build a new society.

## SOCIAL: CLUTCHING ON TO A STRAW

Throughout most of recorded history, it has been "human nature" for individuals to seek collaboration with others when life has been uncertain and the future bleak. It is a survival technique in the midst of a decaying hope to work to improve the future picture when it appears uncertain (Ette, 2001). What happened among the Annang and Ibibio between 1904, when the imperial army known as the West African Volunteer Force arrived, and 1929, when the idea of the Ibibio Welfare Union took off, was of such magnitude as to change their understanding of what it means to be, to belong, and to become. In other words, it affected the very essence of their understanding of what it means to be human. While the old attempted a fight, the young simply gave in and were swept along with the rapid current of changes occurring all around them. But rather than simply be objects of change, they participated and took an active part as agents of change themselves and in the process reached out across old ethnic barriers that resulted in the struggle for a redefinition of identity. As Ekanem (2002) aptly noted, "Whatever comes from without, after a period of a struggled interaction, comes to be shaped by the structure" (p. 127).

The Annang society, especially in the minds of the young and Western educated, had come to be shaped by what was seen as new and civilized. Old boundaries and taboos were now irrelevant and useless, and groups formerly identified as foreign and different were now brought together under the influence of the missionaries and colonialists. The IWU attempted to continue the unifying influence introduced by the bringing together of Ibibio, Annang, and Andoni under the Enyong District experiment before 1914 when it was split. As noted earlier, there was a vacuum in the Annang cosmology. Because the traditional rulers took their authority from the spirit world and such authority was confirmed and communicated through the ancestors, the abolition of that spiritual and social order when the traditional rulers became mere agents of the colonialists challenged the African sense of order and required new linkages in order to make sense of the social world. The IWU was just one example of a structural change made possible by the disturbance of the known social order. It was a desperate attempt at survival and meaning in the midst of impermanence and rapid change.

Ekanem (2002) has written about the activities and lack of cultural sensitivity on the part of the Christian missionaries in Africa who adopted a model of tearing their converts from their roots in order to give them the Christian faith. Thus, the new Christian was not to initiate into the Ekpo cultural society, contract any marriage outside of the church, marry more than one wife, and if the prospective convert had more than one wife before accepting the faith, others were to be sent away in disgrace with no thought of what would happen to their children. The route to conversion has been characterized by Ekanem (2002) as one of "disintegration, degeneration and decomposition" (p. 104). The adoption of this model was informed by racism and the European conviction that the African was incapable of thinking of anything that was not evil (Kenyatta, 1938). Stripped of their bearings and foundations, the IWU represented an attempt by the young to refocus their energies on themselves and their people.

Returning to the religious elements of IWU, the minutes book showed that the Christian religion played an important part early in the life of the organization. The individuals who gathered to form the IWU had lived through the Spirit Movement that swept through the area, and many of them, like one of IWU's presidents, Udoesen Obot, were active participants. To these people, IWU was a continuation of that divine design to fight the kingdom of Satan. In fact, all the deliberations of the organization began with Christian songs and prayers. We have already seen the aims of the organization and maintained that they were reproductions of Wesleyan theology that prescribed social actions as a manifestation of Christian life, but what must be added here is that such theology, though Wesleyan in origin, was Africanized and appropriated to suit the conditions of the Africans in the formation of the IWU.

In this chapter we have argued that the formation of IWU was brought about by the necessity of the Western educated to remain relevant during the early colonial period. We have further argued that rather than see the IWU as an example of the oneness of the people, we miss an important lesson when we fail to examine the historical factors associated with the formation of the organization. If there was a doubt about the symbiotic relationship exhibited between the colonialists and the missionaries in Africa, this chapter has shown a good example of such collaboration. Both the missionaries and the colonial agents believed in the divine duty to save the African; whatever was done, the aim remained the same, and even though they sometimes disagreed, they worked for the benefit of each other.

The Western-educated Africans seemed to have learned the lesson that they were taught well for they saw European education and lifestyle as valuable things to aspire to. Yet the analysis has shown that those who maintained a conspiracy theory and saw the organization more as an instrument of the young usurping power may not be entirely wrong. A future chapter will examine the conspiracy theory further, but for now let us turn our attention and see how the philanthropic and welfare organization became a political pressure group.

*Chapter Seven*

# Power and Politics as Philanthropy

Since the arrival of Western colonialism in Africa, the questions of who is in charge and who makes the rules for the governance of the society have always been thorny ones exacerbated by ancient disagreements and ethnic animosities. Before the advent of the colonial and missionary enterprises, individual ethnic groups dealt with each other as foreign powers without the need to extend powers beyond their borders. As already noted, colonialism changed the political landscape and violently transferred political and economic power from those formerly entrusted with such powers in the precolonial society to individuals with new values. The colonialists appropriated to themselves the right to govern the society but without the responsibilities that accompany power. They collected taxes and made rules without the benefits of citizenship. This chapter will attempt an examination of power as understood and managed not by the colonialists but by the Western-educated elite who wanted power from the colonialists. Shut out from political and economic power despite their Western education, Nigerians formed ethnic organizations. This chapter will examine the process and the evolution of one such organization called the Ibibio Welfare Union (IWU) from its beginnings as a social philanthropy to a political organization.

The foundation for the political activities of the IWU was laid early in its formation by the goals of the organization that sought to unite what they called "the subtribes of Ibibio and Annang." Because no unity or action was possible without the expressed permission of the colonial administration, it meant that the organization would of necessity engage in the politics of the colonial administration. The latter was very concerned with the activities of the Western-educated elites and it did not believe that the IWU was organized for philanthropic reasons, so on August 3, 1929, Mr. M. D. W. Jeffreys, the district officer, accompanied by the deputy resident and headmaster of the Etinan Institute Mr. R. J. Taylor, and Reverend Williams Groves of the Primitive Methodist mission in Ikot Ekpene attended the IWU meeting in Ikot Ekpene (Noah, 1988). At the meeting, Mr. Jeffreys demanded changes to the running of the organization to ensure that its activities were not subversive. Among his demands were that the registration fee be lowered, the proceeding of the meeting made public, financial records kept and made available, and the religious elements kept to a minimum. Other demands included that the colonial official in the area be made aware of the existence of the organization and that he, Mr. Jeffreys be supplied with the minutes book for review and that the organization should consider looking into translating the Bible into their local language (Noah, 1988).

Noah (1988) stated that it was after the colonial agents had satisfied themselves that the organization did not pose a threat that they gave their approval. Soon afterward, the number of membership applications by Europeans increased. It is interesting to note that it was Mr. Jeffreys, the colonial officer, who was more interested in the translation of the Bible into the local vernacular rather than Reverend Groves, who was the missionary. But such was the collusion and common interest between the colonialists and the missionaries in Africa that one advocated for the other.

By its very existence, the IWU had signaled to the colonialists and the missionaries that looking out for the benefits of its members was a political act, and Mr. Jeffreys and Reverend Groves were quite aware of the political implications of its existence and thus were quick to look into the activities of the organization. To understand the motives of Reverend Groves, the missionary, and his interest in policing the activities of the educated Africans, it is perhaps necessary to provide a quick review of the history and practice of the organization that he represented in the missionary enterprise.

## THE ROLE OF THE MISSIONARY

Reverend Groves was a missionary of the Primitive Methodist Missionary Society (PMMS) who arrived in Ikot Ekpene with his wife, Barbara, in 1919. The missionary society dates back to 1807 when two evangelical Methodist preachers, Hugh Borne and William Clowes, began holding open-air "camp meetings" in England. Refusing to desist from such practices considered "improper" by the established Methodist Church, the two were dismissed and the name "primitive" added to the movement. By 1843, the movement formed the Primitive Methodist Missionary Society and sent Missionaries to Canada, New Zealand, and Australia, but by 1870, the attention of the PMMS turned toward Africa and stations were established in Fernado Po, South Africa, and the Upper Zambezi in Central Africa. The PMMS did not establish a station in Nigeria until 1903 when the society began what they called the Southern Nigeria Missions. Mission stations were launched from Fernado Po and saw the establishment of stations at Oron, Jamestown, and Urua Eye. Expansions in these stations brought the PMMS to Ikot Ekpene, Bende, Uzuakoli, and Port Harcourt, the important towns of the period in southern Nigeria.

It is important to note, for our purposes here, that the model of evangelization utilized by the PMMS in the Southern Nigerian Missions was what was known as the Native Teaching Evangelists Model (NTEM), popularly known as each-one-teach-one. The missionaries were responsible for training adherents of the faith in the stations and launching them to the villages and towns to conduct open-air missioning in villages and towns. Therefore this model required training institutes and schools to be established for the training of the evangelists. Therefore, along with the colonialists, the missionaries raised Western education as an ideal to be aspired to by the Africans. Because the missionary enterprise required peace and laws by the colonialists, both enterprises shared a symbiotic relationship in Annangland and maintained a common interest. While the colonialists employed the coercive powers of the colonial empire to quell rebellion, the missionaries worked with the Africans to change hearts and minds.

Such was the arrangement when Reverend Groves attended the meeting of the IWU on June 7, 1929. He discouraged drinking and the serving of alcohol in the meetings, pointing out that such imbibing clouds the mind. Like Mr. Jeffreys, Reverend Groves raised the following points:

All should learn from Dr Aggrey who has acknowledged the benefits of racial harmony illustrated in the black and white keys of the piano.
Urged IWU to teach its members hymns compiled in the vernacular, especially the ones sung in churches.
Urged the organization to stay focus on one project at a time.
Provide children in the area with reading materials in the vernacular before attempting to translate the Bible into the vernacular (contradicting Dr. Jeffrey).
He encouraged sanitary living and work on town planning, complaining that children who have been taught in the mission schools lack models at home to emulate. (Noah, 1988, p. 107)

It was not therefore an accident that following the speech by Reverend Groves to the group, subsequent meetings took on an air of a revival meetings with hymns from the Primitive Hymnal.

## GOOD-SPEAK AND THE POLITICS OF LANGUAGE

Nothing brings controversy and argument among the groups in southern Nigeria like the issue of whose language is better and who has the power to define what the official language should be. Igwara (2001) reminded us that in Nigeria, ethnic identification and by extension language becomes the currency for negotiation and social calculation. As we have seen earlier, the colonialists defined and influenced not only the political landscape but also the linguistic landscape; therefore the colonial experience for the Annang and Africans in general was total in its effect. Colonialism, the subsequent introduction of English as the medium of instruction, and the active promotion of Western education as avenues of wisdom and modernity rendered local languages primitive and backward while promoting the English language, which was seen as the avenue to sophistication and the new life. Those who could speak the English language had access to power.

Notwithstanding this preference, as we have noted before, when the British colonial office set up a commission to recommend local vernaculars as media of instructions at the first few years of primary education at the local levels, the missionaries and colonial administrators quickly recommended the Efik language for the Annangs, Efiks, Eket, Oron, and Ibibios in southeast Nigeria. The bringing together of these formerly autonomous groups and the mistaken notion by the colonialists that they were all one prompted an outcry that fueled many activities to reassert the autonomy of these groups and to communicate their displeasures for being homogenized. The Efik feared losing their place in the colonial regime, while the Ibibios on the other hand appealed to history to claim their superiority over the Efiks. The Annangs, Oro, and Eket on the other hand saw themselves as observers in the dispute. Yet as we shall see, the dispute over whose language was to be adopted as the language of instruction carried a big reward for the language of instruction is often elevated to a higher level as the language of the elite and educated class, thereby giving the language a prestige and its speakers a political advantage.

This lesson was not lost to the IWU's executive and they visited the subject of the colonial education office picking Efik language instead of Ibibio often. At a meeting in Ikot Obong Edong, Ikot Ekpene, attended by Mr. Jeffreys, the president of IWU took advantage of the district officer's presence to give him a lesson in Ibibio history. He told the colonial officer that the Efiks were actually Ibibio from Uruan who were driven away through war from their homes where they fled to Ikon Eto or what is now Creek Town. They were joined by others fleeing from Eket who settled in Obotong. With the European trade, those from Ikon Eto massacred the settlers in Obotong and afterward monopolized the trade with the Europeans. The observable difference in speech, the president continued, is a consequence of intermarriages between the settlers and the neighboring groups on account of the shortage of women, which led to marriages outside of the settler groups.

As if to bolster his argument beyond the simple history, the IWU president demonstrated to his visitors that the Efik language is actually deficient in its vocabulary and depends on conjugations and the corruption of foreign words for its normative categories and "is not a pure language" (Noah, 1988, p. 106). The president provided the following examples: while the Ibibio's name for soap is "otong," the Efik corrupts soap and therefore are able to say "suop" and paper for "babru." The August visitors also learned from the president that "the Efik language was irregular while the Ibibio is regular—as ifono (Ibibio) ifonke (Efik) nkite (Ibibio) nque (Efik). The Ibibio language is pure, being a very ancient language before Christ but Efik is impure, being a slave language" (Noah, 1988, p. 106).

Interestingly, the president used the same language that led to the filing of the suit against Mr. E. N. Amaku and the Ibibio Mainland Association that was earlier discussed in the previous chapter. Because it appeared as if Mr. Jeffreys was not convinced, the president had two more points added to his argument. The Ibibio, he furthered argued, was the language of the majority with 750,000 speakers, whereas Efik only had a mere 30,000 speakers. With a larger population speaking the language, the president felt that Ibibio was robbed of its rightful place as the language of instruction. A second point was the age-old argument of taxation. The president gave a breakdown of the taxes collected by the colonial government in 1928. Of the 85,000 British pounds collected in the area, the president noted that only 5,000 of that amount came from the Efiks, with the Aros and Andonis paying a combined sum of 10,000, while the Ibibios paid a whopping 70,000 (Noah, 1988).

Despite the seemingly solid argument, Mr. Jeffreys and Reverend Groves both suggested that a written literature overrides the history and all the arguments that the Ibibio had about the superiority of their language. They further suggested that writing down something in their language is certainly one way to call attention and recognition to their tongue. This same argument would be used ninety years later in what is now called Akwa Ibom State as the people continue to suffer the effects of colonialism, as we shall see later. With Ibibio chosen as the language of instruction by the educated Ibibios in 1987, the Annang would argue that they should be allowed to use their own language as a medium of instruction in their schools. There is no disagreement that there is a difference in the speech patterns in southern Nigeria in general and in what is now Akwa Ibom in particular. The linguistic difference and ethnic pride has led to claims making. As Farb (1974) noted, the Annangs take pride in their language and just like those in ancient Greece consider it the best in the world. Other languages are considered less clear and those who speak differently are seen as asem usem, literally meaning those who could not be understood. The emphasis is on the verb "asem," which connotes unintelligibility and imprecision for the word "usem" can be used for language. Farb (1974) continued:

> The name Annang means "they who speak wittily upon any occasion." They admire the ability to speak well . . . and pride themselves on their eloquence . . . their youth are encouraged from earliest childhood to develop verbal skills. (pp. 125–26)

Gore and Pratten (2003) have also noted that eloquence and the ability to speak the language well determines selection as a leader in youth organizations. Thus, it is not difficult to see how ethnic identity emerges as an important factor in the Annang society. This pride in linguistic superiority perhaps accounted for the reason that the Annang in the IWU demanded that a proposed magazine of the organization include articles in Annang along with those in Ibibio. This disagreement might have sunk the proposed publication as the Annang refused to accept a magazine published only in another tongue.

## "MATTERS OF VITAL INTEREST"

One of the aims of the IWU was the creation of a forum "to meet from time to time to discuss matters of vital interest" (Noah, 1988, p.74). The inclusion of such a broad aim allowed the organization to keep the door open for the discussion and planning of responses to political issues in the colonial era.

Several things were of interest to members of the IWU, among which were participation in the civil service, education, acculturation, and political power.

In the colonial period in Africa, the rights and value attached to individuals depended on their classification. Mbembe (2001) observed that such arrangement was an extension of the slave culture and practices that existed in the Western world. Whether one had rights and value depended on whether one was white or black. The value of one's labor further defined the individual, thus a teacher, clerk, or clergy was more valuable than a manual laborer in the colonial civil service system. The civilizing enterprise recognized Western education as an agent of social mobility only within limits that cannot be extended beyond race, which was seen as a natural barrier. In fact, the colonial education curriculum was borrowed from the Tuskegee Institute in Alabama in the United States, an institution that was set up to educate the newly freed slaves in what Booker T. Washington called the education of the hand not of the mind (Fafunwa, 1974). Such school subjects in the colonial school curriculum as handwork and nature's study reflected the European understanding of the need and capability of the Africans. Yet a job in the colonial civil service, as already mentioned, was seen as a reward for the acquisition of Western education, which simply was the ability to read and write. It meant that the individual was liberated from the shackles of African primitivity. It was not surprising, given this reality, for Africans to aspire toward the colonial civil service not only because of the perceived benefits but also because of what it meant in terms of individual value and prestige. Yet a glass ceiling existed beyond which no African was allowed. The British colonial administrators allocated to themselves the sole right of administering the area according to the colonial's office directive, and no African was allowed to be a part of the decision-making process.

It became necessary, therefore, given the changes around them for Africans to seek Western education as a way to participate in the new society. As Noah (1988) observed, "The Ibibio Union was an organization which sought to use collective representation to accommodate, resist, modify or manipulate the colonial system" (p. 48). Despite the importance and the willingness of the people to acquire Western education, the imperial administration set the school fee at twelve pounds a year by 1930 for each pupil in the primary school, quite out of reach for the ordinary African. Moreover, the schools in the area were restricted to only a few years and children could go only as far as the fourth grade. The IWU saw the bonding together as a way of addressing this issue with the colonialists. The acquisition of Western education became an issue of ethnic pride through which the organization sought to measure its success. Following the tax riot of 1929 and emboldened by their support for the government on the issue, the IWU president announced plans to ask for the establishment of a middle school in the area. Though the ban on senior grades was later lifted, allowing for middle schools in Ikot Ekpene, Abak, Eket, and Etinan, there still was no secondary school in the area, and this forced children who passed the rigorous entrance examination to wait to be admitted in the nearest secondary school that was in Umuahia several miles away in the Igbo territory. Therefore the IWU saw itself as an advocate for the establishment of a high school in the Annang and Ibibio area. At a meeting at Itu Mr. R. U. Inyang, the then secretary of the IWU, reminded the IWU members that the establishment of a school was not the responsibility of the organization but that of the colonial native administration, but that the IWU was strongly committed to urging the native administration to establish such school (Noah, 1988).

By the end of 1930 serious consideration and discussions had begun about sending individuals abroad to study and establishing a high school in the area. Letters were written to the colonial authorities about plans to establish a middle school. A "college" at Uyo for boys only was proposed. The union rightly discussed the education of women, and some were concerned with the unwillingness of parents to send their female children to school. They urged the IWU to consider establishing a school for girls because the Uyo school would educate only boys. This did not win popular approval, but it was agreed that female education, when considered, be not made "literal education . . . but such that will fit them in all rounds of life, e.g home and children management and to train them in the different kinds of manual or hand work" (Noah, 1988, p. 153). This idea of industrial education for women did not go further; in fact, the union did not pursue the idea of education for women until several years afterward.

## AGITATION FOR POWER

Though the Africans were denied political power in the colonial administration, they continued to press for changes and used whatever opportunities presented themselves to their advantage. As Akpan (1967) observed, the newly educated Africans derived encouragement and inspiration from the realization that the old African society with its traditional ways was disintegrating in the face of the introduction of European culture and governance. They then seized the opportunity to challenge old taboos, religion, and ways of life of the indigenous society. Several methods were employed in this regard.

Ethnic boundaries disappeared as the educated and the young sought out whatever jobs were available in the colonial administration. The Efiks, for example, followed the Presbyterian missionaries into the Ibibio and Annang territories and served as school masters and interpreters, while those from Oron as previously mentioned followed the Primitive Methodist missionaries to Ikot Ekpene and beyond. As a rule, those who had earlier contact with the Europeans and benefited from Western education provided middle- and lower-level manpower. This included the Igbos, Yorubas, Sierra Leoneans, and Liberians who came east and the Efiks and Oron who moved west to Ikot Ekpene. As Akpan (1967) again reminded us, when the traders were added to the number, the number of nonindigenes in Ikot Ekpene, for example, increased tremendously, and it became impossible for the colonialists to ignore them. In Ikot Ekpene, these nonnative Africans along with the native-born united and formed what was called the Ikot Ekpene Society, which became a social networking organization.

Exposed to the global reforms and agitation for freedom that characterized the discourse and intercourse of the pre– and post–World War II, this educated class saw themselves as agents of change by defying old traditions and authorities. No longer tethered to the taboos of the old ways, they mounted challenges and opposition against the African traditional authorities (Akpan, 1967). Because the old ways revolved around the authority of the elders and chiefs, they saw the chiefs as obstacles to progress and openly called for the elimination of their functions. In 1929, for example, at the height of the Women's Riot, the IWU sent letters to the villages without consulting the chiefs. In those letters they characterized the demonstration as the creation of troublemakers and apportioned to themselves the title of "true friends" of the people. The IWU members presented themselves and their new organization to the colonialists as a mouthpiece of the indigenous society and by-passed the authority of the indigenous chiefs. They sought out and placed themselves as adjudicators in conflicts between groups as when they tried and imposed resolution on the Ibiono No. 1 and Ibiono No. 2 dispute in 1937. Rather than rely on the traditional ways, the IWU showed their superior Western education and the advantage of the new method by using the British Intelligence Report and the Ibiono Clan Council Minute Book. This ability to use their education gave them an upper hand against the indigenous traditions and methods. The Christian religion frowned on the functions of the chiefs as priest of the traditional religion and rendered them merely as peddlers of superstitions and agents of darkness. Thus, the chief had a duty as a priest but without any adherents of the faith. They lost their voice on important matters and became irrelevant in a society that they once controlled.

Yet despite the growing power of the new educated class and their claims, they did not represent all in the society. Besides the chiefs and the elders already discussed earlier, "the professional salaried and trading classes," as Sir Bernard Bourdillon, the former governor-general of Nigeria, called them, ignored the peasant class. This resulted in the British colonialists claiming to represent the interests of the peasant class as a way to isolate the African educated class and portray them as selfish.

The Richards Constitution sought to undercut the power of the salaried class by requiring the native authorities to send elected representatives to the central legislature in Lagos. But because those in the native administrations were illiterate and could not function in a body in which the reading and writing of English was a requirement for participation, it opened the door to the educated middle class to become a part of the legislative body and therefore assume political power (Akpan, 1967).

Having tasted power, the IWU slowly began the process of transforming itself. It demonstrated what was already known: that politics could not be divorced from the social issues facing them as a class and as a people. In 1937, with the Annang declining to go to the central legislative assembly in Lagos, Nyong Essien from Uyo volunteered to represent the Annang and Ibibio in 1937 and essentially became a spokesperson for the Annang and Ibibio.

In this chapter, we have examined the role of Western education in shaping the character and function of the early period as well as the work of IWU. It is interesting to note that despite the history of the Efiks as emigrants from Ibibio, the efforts of the middle class in the early colonial period focused on separating them but instead made claims about the Annang who became members of the organization. The latter became preferred as the in-group while the former, perhaps because of the Amaku case, were made outsiders. It goes to show that IWU, as already argued, was not an ethnic organization in the true sense of the word. What was seen as an ethnic organization was merely a response to the immediate situation. In the next chapter, we shall examine group relationships and dynamics as a result of membership in the organization. IWU slowly, as a result of circumstance and in response to issues, transformed itself into a political force despite the efforts of the colonialists to check its activities.

## Chapter Eight

# Group Relationships and Dynamics

Though ethnic conflict in precolonial African society cannot be ruled out, it was exacerbated and affected by the European colonial administrative machinery in the colonies (Obioha, 1999). In the foregoing chapter we saw an example of the introduction of conflict between the Efiks and Ibibio brought about by a colonial policy of asking for public comments and memoranda for the selection of one particular dialect among many in a multiethnic society without a deep consideration of the history and effect of such policy. This ill-conceived policy and disregard for the history of the area led to a reawakening of a latent conflict between the two groups.

This chapter will examine the relationships of the different ethnic groups that belonged to Ibibio Welfare Union (IWU). The goal is to attempt an analysis of the dynamics of ethnicity and organizational goal with a view to discovering how ethnicity affected the workings of the organization. Because the approach is purely historical and the method a secondary analysis, it is safe to assume that derived conclusions may be flawed; but on the other hand, an examination of the records of who made what decision and the rationale for making such decisions in the face of what was known to be true or not true can reveal a lot about how these early pioneers worked together and what motivated them to overcome ethnocentrism if any. If the reverse is true and they were guided mostly by ethnocentric biases, perhaps we too can learn a lesson or two from their experience. Let us begin with current assumptions in contemporary analysis of the period under consideration.

Contemporary historians with the benefit of hindsight have tended to romanticize the history of IWU and saw the era as the finest epoch in group relations and organization (Noah, 1988, 1987b; Udoma, 1988). This romanticized past is not only the purview of historians. In a ceremony held recently to induct Sir Emem Akpabio, the pioneer president of Ati-Annang into the

Mboho Mkparawa Ibibio organization, the president of Mboho Mkparawa Ibibio was quoted in the news media as saying,

> In the spirit of the legendary Ibibio State Union of 1928 which fosters peace, love, unity and togetherness, when all present Akwa Ibom, irrespective of ethnic lineage, were one in the Ibibio family, the Mboho Mkparawa Ibibio the foremost socio-cultural organisation in the state has inducted Sir Emem Akpabio as a member of the association. (*Akwa Ibom State Government News Online*, n.d.)

Yet a detailed study of the record and particularly the minutes book revealed that the professional salaried class and the traders that made up IWU were not immune to the issues and problems posed by ethnicity. Brought together across traditional ethnic and group lines by necessity, these individuals who were beneficiaries and products of Western education saw themselves as agents of change whose best chances for dealing with the colonialists was cooperation. They also believed that their own traditional and indigenous culture was lower on the cultural continuum than the European culture. With a decentralized and heavily fragmented society during colonialism, the idea of gathering whatever was left under a single organization and assuming the role of a mouthpiece of the society was irresistible. Because the salaried class could speak the new language and understood the new rulers, all that was required was convincing the colonialists that there was a group they could deal with and who were different from the traditional chiefs. The group also saw the missionary enterprise as agents of civilization. When the leopard killings occurred in Southern Annang in the 1940s, for example, the Ibibio Union blamed the killings on the ineffectiveness of the missionaries in the area and described the activities of the mission as "pouring water on a duck's back" (Report, 1947). To the members of the IWU, old superstitions of the indigenous culture kept alive due to the ineffectiveness of the European missionaries in the area were to blame for the murders and so the union went around the area preaching against such evil (Nwaka, 1986).

No evidence exists of a centralized governing structure between the groups in southern Nigeria before colonialism, as we have noted. Unlike the western and northern parts of the country where the Oba and Emir ruled respectively over large territories, the Igbos and most groups in the Niger delta did not evolved into a mega-state system. Yet this did not imply, as many Western amateur ethnographers maintained, that the society was without a governing structure where everyone was a king (Uzoigwe, 2004). Far from southeastern Nigeria being a pan-Ibibio governing structure, communities recognized consanguine relationships and exploited such relationships into governing structures and systems that served them well. Thus, the Annang recognized Iman as already described and organized governing structures to suit such relationships. The Ibibios also did the same as the Igbos, and relationships across these lines first acknowledge sameness among groups. Therefore the Annang recognized and dealt with other Annang Imans differently from their Igbo and Ibibio neighbors. The inability to understand the workings of this system was the main reason that indirect rule introduced by British colonialism failed in the south but worked well in the northern part of the country (Noah, 1987a; Akpan, 1967).

Group relationships in the colonial period could be characterized as that which exists between captured people (Mbembe, 2001.) Brought together under the shackles of colonialism and with the coercive force of the colonialists, old divisions and animosities were not tolerated by the British colonialists and the missionaries who understood very little about the people that they ruled over. To the colonialists, all Africans were savages who needed to be tamed, and to the missionaries all Africans stood in need of the saving grace of the European God. The missionaries saw themselves as acting on God's behalf to save the African savages. The most important thing for both the colonialists and the missionaries was "civilization," the very definition of which only the Europeans knew. There were, however, certain requirements that could be used as benchmarks to measure the civilizing influence and to determine who was civilized; these included the ability to speak, read, and write the English language, acceptance of the Christian religion, and changes in attire from the indigenous to European.

## THE SOCIAL AND POLITICAL CENTER OF THE STRUGGLE

Using the yardsticks mentioned here, it was not surprising that those who came to work for the colonial state in Annangland were individuals who had had the opportunity to acquire these elements of the European culture. Akpan (1967) observed that these educated natives saw their own indigenous culture as "unprogressive and inefficient." As indicated earlier, some of these were individuals who were from areas with early contact with the Western world. In this analysis, we shall use Ikot Ekpene as the basis of analysis for as Alexis de Tocquille wrote more than 150 years ago, the story of a township can tell us more about a people than monarchies. Yet he reminded us that the freedom of a town and its greatness are fragile. The story of the town and the analysis of its history can reveal something about those who lived in it and who called it home. It is the centerpiece of the cultural history of a people and can, on examination, reveal a record of the daily lives of those who lived in it. Ikot Ekpene was the center of European colonial activity in the mainland area of southeast Nigeria and by the time of the formation of the Ibibio Welfare

Union in 1929 had achieved an international status with foreign companies and individuals from various places in the area. The town as Nair (1972) noted was considered the political and cultural capital of both the Ibibio and Annang. By 1919 trade with Europeans opened up as the town became an administrative center. The following companies had posts and stores in the town: John Holt Cooperative Wholesale Society, Paterson Zochonos (PZ), G. B. Olivant, and the Compagnie Francaise de L'Afrique Occidentals. The establishment of these companies resulted in exodus from the surrounding areas and made Ikot Ekpene a vibrant metropolis. In 1937, the colonial administration built the main market and separated those who sold imported European goods from indigenous articles. A slaughterhouse was added to allow for the inspection of meat (Ette, 2009).

In Ikot Ekpene just before World War I, the Sierra Leoneans came to work among the Annang, as did the Liberians. The Efiks also came as school teachers and clerks as well as the Yorubas and Igbos. As the Ibibio Welfare Union minutes showed, the Efiks, Igbos, and Yorubas treated the Ibibios and the Annang with contempt because these groups had very little or no education and could only serve as domestic servants. Along with other Africans in the area the Efiks, Yorubas, and Igbos formed the African Club in Ikot Ekpene where they displayed their European taste in food and music. The salaried and the business classes got together, socialized, and discussed issues of common interest in this organization. Pushed out of the circles of those closed to the colonial power, the indigenous class had nowhere to go. The formation of the IWU was therefore a reaction to the activities of this organization. It followed the success of the Ibibio Mainland Association in confronting the Amaku insult at Calabar and presented itself as a forum for the indigenous class.

With the formation of IWU, formerly different groups came together voluntarily unlike the forced marriage that the colonialists imposed on them earlier, when all in the area were either made a part of the Enyong Division or later as the Ikot Ekpene Division. The conditions under which they came together voluntarily raised several interesting questions. Why did Udosen Obot not align with the Igbos and the Efiks in the Ikot Ekpene Association but chose to work with James Udo Eka in the formation of a new organization? And why did the members of IWU from Ikot Ekpene give a lot of power to their compatriots from Uyo including moving the venue of the earlier meetings to Uyo even though Ikot Ekpene was a more popular town back then?

Besides the reasons advanced earlier in this chapter, two theories have been advanced to answer this question. The first can be described as Machiavellianism and the other as charisma. The former maintained mostly by the new Annang educated and radical elites who were born after the activities of IWU saw the union as an arsenal of certain individuals for the destruction of Annang generally and Ikot Ekpene in particular, while the latter is maintained by the more moderate elites saw the union as a tool for good given the circumstances at the time. Before we examine these theories further in the light of what we now know, it is important to give a brief review of the town at the time.

Ikot Ekpene was a cultural and administrative capital and had foreign departmental stores as already noted. It attracted so many people from different areas. It had a public library established by the colonialists and nobody in the colonial administration could afford to ignore the town. Kaanan Nair (1972) stressed the importance of the town to the British colonialists by pointing out that when a road linking Owerri and Calabar was to bypass the town, the British abandoned the idea in favor of one linking Owerri and Eket in order to bring the town into the loop (Nair, 1972). Thus, the town was very important and forced all in the area to go to it for dealings with the colonial government. This fact was known to the indigenes and so arose the saying *Atime Iköt Akpene, atime uchölö*, meaning whoever stays away from Ikot Ekpene misses a festival. It was a place for night life, business, trade, politics, and learning. The Europeans divided the town into European quarters and the African section. It was there that the educated Africans played tennis and lived in luxury. The place could be located in all maps at a time when other places in what is now Akwa Ibom State were mere villages not known to the outside world. Ikot Ekpene was an envy to others who could only imagine its nice roads and busy nightlife. How those who joined the union could sell their town and hand over their prominent place to others has been a subject of debate among some Annang elements. This is where the Machiavellian theory arises.

## MACHIAVELLIANISM

Niccolo Machiavelli (1469–1572) was an Italian politician who advocated the use of cunning and deceit as tools to gain political power (Zastrow, 1989). Cut off and made irrelevant in the new political structure, James Udo Eka and others saw the formation of a union as a way to become relevant in the new era. Ikot Ekpene was gaining popularity in the colonial era and many were drawn to the town by the establishment of administrative headquarters. One wonders why Udosen Obot, an Ikot Ekpene native, saw the formation of a new organization where others became leaders as an answer to what was happening in his hometown. Yet the struggle for identity and meaning in a new era meant devising something different. The two men were facing not only the British colonialists but were also up against other African elements who saw them as less important. As was pointed out earlier, the Sierra Leoneans and Liberians who served the middle-level manpower needs of the colonial government used the indigenes of the area only as domestic servants. The African struggle as demonstrated here has always not been with the West alone but also with fellow Africans who are closer to power. Under the omnipotent eyes of the colonialists who did not tolerate dissent, a welfare organization away from the center of power became the best approach.

The organization rested on the assumption of Mr. James Udo Eka that all in Ibibio and Annang could be classified as Ibibio. He told those newly invited to the meeting at Uyo that the purpose of calling together the salaried and the trading classes to the meeting was the discussion of matters of common interest (Noah, 1988). If all who could understand the Ibibio dialect could be so classified, then those from Oron, Eket, and the Efiks who left Ibibioland to what is now the cross-river are were prominently absent. In fact, those not selected for membership were not allowed initially to be present at the deliberation of the organization. In 1930, for example, A. E. Idiok from Ibeno, who attended the meeting of IWU, was ordered out of the meeting and the notes that he was taking were confiscated and ordered to be destroyed. The question that he had to answer as a condition of attendance at the meeting was "do you like to be called Ibibio?" Though Mr. Idiok did not object to the designation, the members present demanded an affirmation from his people. Yet it should have been clear to the IWU members that those from Ibeno did understand the Ibibio dialect and could also speak it. Yet the Annang who attended the meeting sat through the introduction and only later did the conveners clarify the purpose of the organization as the creation of unity between Ibibio and Annang. The membership of the organization presented some problems and seemed to run counter to the purpose of its formation. The one shilling monthly membership fee made it too expensive then for the nonsalaried class to become members even though the purpose was given as lifting "the race." Mr. M. D. W. Jeffreys, the district officer, had to intervene and suggested a five shilling subscription annually to make it easier for more people to join. At a shilling a month the IWU membership dues were more expensive than the Europeans Civil Servant Club in Nigeria and more than the tax paid by each individual to the colonial government according to Mr. Jeffreys. Thus, the IWU became elitist and excluded those of the nonsalaried class that could have offered good suggestions on ethnic and historical relations. As Chief Udo Akpabio of Ukana Ikot Ntuen complained to Reverend W. T. Groves in 1930, "the old men and chiefs are much poorer than the young men" (p. 57). With the poverty of the older generation and with very high membership dues in what they considered an alien organization, the IWU became a forum for the young educated men.

Another issue in the Machiavellianism theory is the lack of decentralization in the administration of the union until a protest from the Ikot Ekpene members forced what can be described as a mini decentralization. Though the idea for the organization began in Ikot Ekpene, the location of the meeting was moved to Uyo even though more of the people lived in Ikot Ekpene at the time. This distance led to problems with transportation, as already mentioned. Yet in spite of this obvious problem, a decentralization that would have required meetings at separate locations proved hard to adopt. It was only the insistence of the Ikot Ekpene members and a threat of boycott that led to the adoption of what was to become "local branches." However, the loyalty of the Annang group in the organization could be seen from a report by Udosen Obot, who at a meeting of the union in Abak sought permission of the organization to ask the colonial administration for a superior court. The union refused to grant this request and instead asked Mr. Obot to request for a magistrate court that "would benefit all districts" (Noah, 1988, p. 138). A few lessons quickly emerge from this episode besides the loyalty of Mr. Obot to the organization. Why was the union afraid to grant the permission? To answer this question, it is necessary to look at the functions of the courts at the time. The British allowed native courts to function but appointed magistrates to handle appeals from these native courts. A superior court was higher in the hierarchy of the colonial judicial system and would have allowed Ikot Ekpene to maintain its importance as the administrative capital. The argument as summarized by Mr. Obot was that Ikot Ekpene was what was called a "second-class township" and therefore was deserving of a superior court. Mr. Obot sought the permission of the IWU because according to him, he saw the use of the name of the union as adding weight to his request. The matter was seen as not benefiting every division in the area and the request was in turn framed as all divisions needing a magistrate court and not Ikot Ekpene needing a superior court. With this decision, Ikot Ekpene began losing its importance after the union had demonstrated to the colonialists that they were allies following the women's riot. The writing of letters and admonitions in the letters calling the organizers of the riots "foolish" and "troublemakers" provided evidence to the colonialists that the union was a trusted ally and a good mouthpiece of the Annang and Ibibio.

The Ikot Ekpene group after the decentralization of IWU meetings had sought and accepted an affiliation with the Ibibio Mainland Association (IMA) at Calabar. This was the group that successfully led the E. N. Amaku case. The Ikot Ekpene branch adopted a name known as the "Ikot Ekpene Hope Rising Club" (Noah, 1988, p. 98). When a report was filed at a meeting of the IWU about the intention of Ikot Ekpene members to pay membership dues to the

IMA, the former objected to the split and argued for Ikot Ekpene members to remain part of the IWU. A split of Ikot Ekpene members could have substantially weakened the IWU in 1929 because most of the active members at the time were from Ikot Ekpene and were financially more secure than their counterparts in Uyo. Ikot Ekpene members were forced to stay in the union with no apparent benefit beyond "unity." Yet the work on unity was not apparent when the union failed to intervene in matters affecting people from Ikot Ekpene and the mistreatment of Annang traders at Ifiayong (Noah, 1988, p. 148). Two incidents were noted in the minutes book and the union was blamed for not intervening in both cases. The first one is that of one Mr. Harrison whose truck was involved in an accident at Ikot Ekpene. Some members of the union blamed the nonintervention of the union, which led to the case going to court with a great expenditure of funds. Members also complained that Annang traders were treated unfavorably at Ifiayong and despite complaint to the union nothing was done (Noah, 1988). The union, however, was quick to levy two pounds sterling on each village in order to build a teacher training college at Uyo.

The leadership of Mr. Obot, a personal friend and former co-worker of Mr. Eka, may also be cited as another example of the use of Machiavellianism. As noted earlier, Mr. Obot came out of the Spirit Movement that swept across the area early in the colonial period. He had worked with the Primitive Methodist mission but got swept along with the Spirit Movement and lost his relationship with the missionaries. He began an African independent church and had very little formal education beyond the ability to read and write. He was later elected the president of the IWU and saw his new role naively as that of saving his people. Under his leadership, he allowed himself to be manipulated and even when others lost interest he carried on. He assumed the position of president of the organization when the first president Mr. Harrison was kicked out of office and accused of "leaking union secrets." Under Mr. Obot's leadership, the meetings of the IWU were to be rotated and moved from Uyo that had become a permanent secretariat. An attendance and a ledger register were also purchased, allowing the union to keep track of both attendance and the payment of dues. Opening prayers were replaced by three minutes of silence to satisfy the complaints of the Catholics who objected to the Protestant prayers. The union was also registered during his tenure.

Though some positive developments could be attributed to Mr. Obot's leadership, there were a few things that he did wrong. He used his position to give the people a false hope when he told people in Ikot Ekan in 1930 that the union could work with the colonialist in reducing the school fees from twelve pounds (Noah, 1988, p. 119). Though it was a good recruitment line, the fact remained that the union had no such power.

It is interesting that the IWU rejected the advice of Mr. Jeffreys to make the organization a representative body in which delegates could have deliberated the decisions of the body with few general meetings to affirm the decisions of such representatives. Despite the enormous hardships involved with transportation, the union took other advice of Mr. Jeffreys but rejected a representative body in which all the branches could have had the same vote. It is also of note that the IWU concentrated its efforts in Ikot Ekpene and Uyo, drawing people from the former to the latter before extending its influence and recruiting members from Itu, Etinan, Eket, and what is now Ikot Abasi; as a certain Pastor Joseph observed at a meeting of IWU in Ikot Ekan, "The people from Eket and Opobo are not here, all parts of Ibibio have to be present in this meeting in order to confirm what is to be done" (Noah, 1988, p. 123).

No other issue in the life of the union is as sensitive as the establishment of a high school in Ikot Ekpene. With the building of a teacher training college at Uyo, the union rejected the proposal to build a high school at Ikot Ekpene and instead called for the establishment of a primary school. Though a high school was subsequently built despite the opposition of some in the union, the issue remained contentious and after the dissolution of the union the Annang renamed the school "State College," eliminating the mention and reference to Ibibio in keeping with the views of some that have rejected the Ibibio identity.

## CHARISMA

The second theory that is not a conspiracy theory but represents the manifest goal of the association sought to unite the Annang and Ibibio for a common good given the circumstances in which they found themselves. While the Machiavellianism theory can be described as latent and remained the unstated goal, the manifest goal was clearly spelled out in the minutes book of the association that has survived and been made available. The stated purpose and goals of the organization had already been listed and discussed in previous chapters; here we shall concern ourselves with the implementation strategies to achieve such goals.

Shut out from participation and opportunities in the colonial administration, the salaried and trading class sought relevance and organized to gain power and the right to be heard and be represented. The only means of participation was therefore for the educated class to leave their areas of origin and move to centers of economic and political power. These "expatriate natives" as Akpan (1967) called them needed the cooperation of the indigenes in these centers of power to gain attention. It was therefore inevitable that those natives who were influential needed to be coopted and brought into the conversation. Thus, Udosen Obot with his history of dealings with the missionaries and colonialists and his position in the Spirit Movement in Ikot Ekpene became a clear and natural choice. Let us now turn our attention to the practices of the union in order to examine the charisma theory.

The manifest goal of unity was pursued with vigor until the issue of education and the building of a high school in Ikot Ekpene brought disagreements. This was further exacerbated when the members disagreed on approaches to be taken toward dealing with the Man-Leopard murders in Annangland. Between 1943 and 1948, a series of unsolved murders, as many as two hundred, occurred in southern Annang and the Annang-speaking areas of what was then Opobo (Nwaka, 1986; Pratten, 2007). Opinions differed as to who was responsible for the murders. Despite a strong effort by the colonial administration to solve the murders including public hangings, the murders continued unabated. Several theories were advanced to explain this event, prominent among which were three: (1) executions by the Ekpe secret society disguising them as real leopard killings; (2) private random killing by a serial killer or killers; or (3) killings by a real leopard that had developed a taste for human flesh (Nwaka, 1986). The colonial administration maintained that the killings were done by humans and therefore they held onto the first possibility. In a letter to a member of the House of Commons who inquired about the killings in 1947, the governor of Nigeria wrote,

> The real motive behind all the murders is ritual. It is believed that the murders are instigated by the members of the Idiong Society in order to obtain human flesh and organs of the body as offerings to the Idiong Juju, and for the preparation of various and complex charms . . . to obtain these the members of the society and those of the Leopard Society, who are the former agents, encourage and counsel the commission of murder as the only means of settling a grievance, real or imaginary, and afford the murderers every assistance in the perpetration of the crime. (Quoted in Nwaka, 1986, p. 445)

The Ibibio Welfare Union delved into the matter and presented itself as an arbiter between the colonial administration and the Annang people. Though the arbitration took on the combined elements of Christianity and traditional religion and appeared to help the situation, it was the collective punishment method and prohibition of the Idiong cult that divided the opinion of the members. The organization was divided between the pro- and anti-Idiong factions. While some agreed with the banning of the Idiong society by the colonial government, others led by Dr. Udo Udoma wanted the secret cult restored as it was the most prestigious and most powerful of the indigenous secret societies. Its main function in the Annang tradition was for divination and its connection to the murders was very controversial and was based on the confession of some people that Idiong members paid for human organs to use in ritual practices. The anti-Idiong members of the IWU led by the then secretary Mr. U. U. Usen, who worked as a government interpreter, supported the ban, and not surprisingly Usen was honored by the colonial government with a certificate of honor for his efforts in ending the murders before his death in 1949 (Nwaka, 1986). The disagreement over the high-handedness of the colonial response to the murders brought accusations and factions into the union. Though both the pro- and anti-Idiong factions employed oaths and Christian exhortations as tools to deal with the murders, they disagreed on the continued ban of the Idiong secret society. The anti-Idiong faction not surprisingly prevailed, and the Idiong cult remained banned because the Christian missionaries and the colonialists wanted no less. The pro-Idiong faction felt wounded and the claim of the union to speak with one voice was forever shattered. Additionally, this disagreement was further interpreted along ethnic lines. The Annang members felt that their Ibibio compatriots did not wish them well and saw the issue through the Annang and Ibibio divide. The pro-Idiong group had a good argument for their position and called the Idiong cult a "purely religious institution of distinction . . . a dignity which is as innocent and harmless as it is colourful" (quoted in Nwaka, 1986, p. 431). They argued in a letter to the colonial government that the activities of the Idiong cult were not different from those of the Christian sects that claimed to see visions and cure diseases. Despite these arguments, the anti-Idiong faction stood their ground and a disagreement between Annang members and those from Ibibio on this issue affected the unity of the organization. Thus, it is reasonable to argue that the organization worked for the good of the community regardless of the source of the problem.

The effort to elevate the position of the Annang and Ibibio group relative to other groups in Nigeria could be seen in the work of the organization in awarding scholarships and advocating for the establishment of schools in the area. Several individuals benefited from the scholarship scheme launched by the union, but as already noted, the union fell short in including women in its programs. Other goals such as preserving honor, improving manners, being good and useful, creating feelings of love for what is beautiful, sympathizing with those afflicted, and so on were too broad to be of use for the purpose of quantifying its effectiveness and evaluating its achievement and read like a page in a church catechism. Given such observation and the inability to concretize the objective of the union, it is not an accident that those who could not see the benefit and achievement of the union among the Annang tend to subscribe more to the latent goal rather than the manifest one. How, for example, was the Annang honor upheld, they asked? How and in what ways were the feelings of love created when events showed the reverse? Yet the fact remains that contrary to some views, several achievements could be credited to the union. But whether those events in themselves justify its creation and membership for the Annang remains debatable.

Let us examine then some practices of the union and see how the early members implemented the goals they set out to accomplish. This analysis will deal with the early years of the union, and as usual will use the available minutes as evidence of ethnic cooperation or the lack of it.

As stated earlier, the union made efforts to exclude the Efiks who historically could trace their origin to Ibibioland. The organization was therefore not a true ethnic organization. In the first meeting of the organization at Uyo in 1928, the union entertained complaints from individuals against those referred to as "Calabarians" meaning the Efiks in Lagos. We have already discussed the issues and conflicts with the Efiks stemming from the E. N. Amaku memo and the selection of Efik as the medium of instruction in the schools. These events along with the posture of members of the union discredited the assumption that the Ibibio Welfare Union was truly an ethnic Union.

The by-laws of the organization banned the use of individual ethnicity in the affairs of the union. No member was permitted to use ethnic and group claims as arguments and justifications for actions within the union. Thus, membership meant surrendering one's ethnicity. The by-law states, "Every member of the Union should understand that he is a member of the Ibibio Welfare Union and not of any individual subtribes" (Noah, 1988, p. 86). Ironically, the very name of the union represented a normative category and proclaimed that all belonged to a single ethnic group. The rule essentially banned the use of other names and sought to create hegemony. This ban on other identities was further strengthened in 1936 banning publications and reports in the media that are not authorized by the union. In the same year, a system of unified employee acceptance was adopted banning the Ibibio Welfare Union districts from discriminating employees of the colonial native administration who hailed from other IWU districts. With the adoption of this rule, native expatriates moved with ease from rural to urban areas and settled with ease and without fear of being discriminated against in areas where they were nonnatives. Thus, Ikot Ekpene that was the administrative capital saw movements of individuals to the urban center.

## THE EKPO MASQUERADE SOCIETY

While the Ibibio Welfare Union represented an attempt by the educated elite to work with the colonial government, the Ekpo Masquerade Society, on the other hand, was the indigenous opposition group whose members were mostly uneducated in the Western tradition. Members refused to accept the colonial structure and defied colonial laws. In this section, I will reproduce a piece that the author shared in a listserv with some academics on culture in 2010 because it is relevant to the discussion in question.

The idea of putting on costumes to dance and the assumption of a different character during such outings seems to be universal in the area of public entertainment. However, among the Annang of southeast Nigeria, those who were so accoutered assume more than character that went beyond the physical to the spiritual. Members of various associations assume that they were from the world of the spirits who have returned to administer justice to those who were uninitiated and those who violated the rules of social norms. Different associations had different rules and targeted certain groups, often women and those who were too poor to initiate into the particular organization. In this brief analysis, we will examine the history of the masquerade movement among the Annang, noting the functions of the associations and controversy with colonialism in each period. The main aim is to elucidate the relevance and importance of the organization during colonialism. In the process, we seek to organize and separate facts from fiction.

There are several associations in the general classification that are often referred to as masquerades among visitors to Annang villages. It is obvious that the term "masquerade" was a European designation and was brought by the traders who visited West Africa in the seventeenth century. The word itself comes from the French *mascarade*, with the variants of *mascarata* in Italian and *mascarada* in Spanish. In all three languages, it refers to an assembly or party of people wearing masks and dancing for fun. Bell (2014) sees the term as meaning "the representation of alternate identities." However, what the early Europeans saw in West Africa were not the usual partygoers in mask. Those who adorned the masks that they saw had specific functions to perform in the African society. The idea of putting on masks was common throughout West Africa. The African masquerades were in fact secret societies that at various times functioned as investment clubs, judicial councils, execution clubs, and plunderers (Pratten, 2007).

The Ekpo society is said to have originated in what became known as Sierra Leone today and spread throughout the West African region (Pratten, 2007). It was originally part of ancestor worship. Like all religions, it became syncretized and took on elements of indigenous cultures as it spread eastward. Among the Annang, the original worship element was retained and animal sacrifice became an integral part of the cult. Local materials and plants were added as part of the costume and the weapon used by the masqueraders reflected indigenous taste. The Annang chose to indulge in the masquerade revelry in the months between the planting and harvesting season, which falls between May and October to accommodate the need to care for the farm and the crops (Messenger, 1957). As a rule, the practice ends before the harvest period. In the original practice, the ancestors were said to take on characteristics of the spirit world and returned to the land of the living to protect and administer justice during critical times. Because the important elements of the cult were controlled by those with political power, the sharing of the deliberations of the organization became secret and made available only to those who could afford to pay the initiation fees. Because the required fees were exorbitant, it follows that only those with means in the society could join. This practice further made the Ekpo society a secret one. Like all organizations in which those at the top appropriate great power to themselves, those at the Ekpo society made the initiation an investment scheme. New initiates were made to pay and such payments were divided up among the existing hierarchy according to rank and money invested. Such a practice opened the door for corruption and eventually became the source of friction between the Christian missions and the Ekpo society members before World War I. As young men converted to Christianity, such new converts were discouraged from initiating in the Ekpo secret society by European missionaries. The resulting lack of new initiates deprived the Ekpo leaders of their source of wealth and was often the source of conflict between the Christian missions and the Annang traditional society (Pratten, 2007). We shall return again to the conflict between the Christian missions and the Ekpo society, but for now let us turn our attention to the colonialists and how they dealt with this secret society.

## EKPO AND THE CLASH OF VALUES

Nothing in the Annang society was untouched by European colonialism. As was mentioned earlier, those Europeans who came to Annangland in the service of the crown were influenced by the evolutionary theories of the Victorian period (Messenger, 1957). They were not trained ethnographers and their mission was neither the cataloging of Annang culture nor the preservation of the same. They came for the building of the colonial empire and what they saw in the words of Perham (1936) were considered "backward . . . stupid and cruel" (p. 9). Everything in the African society was filtered through this need for peace in the course of building the British colonial empire. Yet the activities of the Ekpo society would bring the colonialist face to face with this powerful group and even threatened the peace that the colonialists thought they had secured.

As Pratten (2007) again noted, there was a certain ambiguity by the colonialists about how to deal with the Ekpo secret society. Some of the colonial agents who were exposed to the hierarchical structure of rulership in other colonial stations were inclined to look at Ekpo as an administrative agent, while others considered it the usual African backwardness and problem. This latter group was more likely to regard the cult as an armed and lawless group of men. The clash between colonial agents and the Annang according to Messenger (1957) was a result of the British concept of justice and their understanding of Christian morality. As the Ikot Ekpene colonial district officer Mr. M. D. W. Jeffreys lamented in 1956, the administration of the colony of Nigeria was to be done according to native law and custom provided it is "not repugnant to natural justice, equity and good conscience," yet natural justice as understood by the agents meant Christian ethics. Seen from this lens, the Ekpo secret society proved to be an anathema. For the Annang, the imposition of other values by the colonialists who were seen as outsiders and invaders became difficult to accept, for as Mbembe (2001) reminded us, the reappropriation of power under colonialism was not merely institutional but also occurred in two other spheres, namely the material and imaginary. The interference by the colonialists robbed the Ekpo members of the benefits of membership as already mentioned, but more than this it disrupted the Annang imagination. Many feared the anger of their neglected gods and refused to accept the end of an era. It is not therefore a surprise that the history of the Ekpo society and its contact with colonialism in Annang is a story of defiance and a refusal to accept change. Members of the society saw a loss of power and were forced to submit to a new authority that refused to acknowledge the importance of the Ekpo society. Yet the judicial decisions of the new system were not always favorable to the Ekpo members. There is evidence that most of the acts of defiance from the Ekpo members came out of their grievances with the new system. Some villages attempted to reject the new system and punished any chief that cooperated with the colonialists. Masked Ekpo in Ikot Idiong, Ukanafun, for example, attacked their chief in 1917 and destroyed the court house. They accused the chief of violating Ekpo law and allowing a foreign judicial system into the village controlled by Ekpo (Pratten, 2007).

Many of the Ekpo members saw the collapse of the familiar and the rise of corruption under the new colonial system. Yet the Ekpo society itself was also corrupt and depended on threat and extortion on noninitiates. Messenger (1957) reported that though the British banned swearing on Mbiam and the use of Ukang as investigative tools, they introduced swearing on the Christian Bible before the start of judicial proceedings. The people did not take such oaths seriously, and those who sat as jurors were easily bribed. The guilty under this new system were often allowed to go free, while those who had power and money to navigate the new system took advantage of it and corrupted the system. The Annang men were particularly irked by the new rule that outlawed the refund of the bride price following divorce or the mocking of the custom by awarding a penny by the British courts as a refund of dowry following a divorce. Punishment for crimes changed overnight such that theft meant imprisonment instead of being shamed in the marketplace. Imprisonment carried little stigma in the community and the convicts returned to the community and reestablished their positions (Pratten, 2007). Crimes that carried the death penalty such as adultery and incest became minimized and offenders were given little or no fines. Given this background, the men saw it as a responsibility to revive the old Ekpo practice and to reassert their authority.

The Ekpo society itself was known for violence. Pratten noted that violence permeated the society such that noninitiates were forced to join through intimidation and assault. The Ekpo society led people to believe that wounds inflicted by Ekpo came from the spirit world and must be expunged and cleansed through initiation into the Ekpo society. Because the incentive to be violent came from recruiting new members, it served the interests of the Ekpo leaders to encourage such violence because the initiation fees were shared. Assaulting noninitiates became the most important function of the masked men during Ekpo outings. There were incentives given to those who had assaulted noninitiates and had thus brought in new members. Such masked men were given the right to carve new mask and were awarded eagle feathers to wear as a badge of recognition as part of their costume (Pratten, 2007). The Ekpo society might have once been a force for good in Annang society, but by the early part of the 1900s, it was corrupted by greed. Perhaps this perception might have figured into an annual report written by the Abak district commissioner that described the society as lawless. Forced into obscurity and irrelevance, the Ekpo society faced many enemies.

In this chapter, we have further examined the goals of the Ibibio Welfare Union within the context of policy and practice in the organization and have paid particular attention to ethnicity and ethnic relations within the organization. Two theories have been examined to illuminate the role of the organization. Though a lot remained to be said about the role of the Ibibio Welfare Union, the fact remains that the contribution of the union to issues affecting Annang in the pre–civil war Nigerian society remains controversial. While some Annang have seen the organization as a force for good, others have tended to see it as a conspiracy that has contributed to the demise of the Annang ethnic group in Nigeria economically and politically. There is, however, no doubt that like any human organization, the Ibibio Welfare Union did certain things right and contributed to the development of the society given the circumstances of the time. Although arguments could also be made to the contrary, it must be borne in mind that all human organizations stand under such judgments. It does seem that some writers have objected to the assertion of the Ibibio Welfare Union as an economic and political agent of progress (Nwaka, 1986). The coming of the colonialists brought several changes to Annangland and its people. Faced with new realities, the people entered into new relationships and agreements. They responded to events in their societies brought on by new situations in their history. Such changes have altered how they see themselves and have also altered their assigned identities. The chapter has further argued that the Ekpo society was an agent of opposition and defiance. Given these new realities, the question of identity naturally arises and will form the subject of the next chapter.

*Chapter Nine*

# The Identity Question

There is a certain truth to the idea that the search for one's identity can be seen as the defense of what Paul Horwitz (2007) calls the true self. Yet the concept of identity since its coinage in 1919 by Tausk has remained important but ambiguous in some disciplines but frequently seen as "a psychic structure" in others (Akhtar, 1999). It involves a subjectivity through which one sees the self in the world and through which one claims a sense of belonging with the self and others. It is what makes us unique and different from others. Social scientists have generally seen group identity as the product of what is transmitted through the generations and by which whole groups identify with and through which they claim a sense of belongingness. It is more properly seen through the eyes of the group and cannot be imposed from the outside. Yet among Africans, the idea of ethnic identity was seen through the lenses of the colonialists. Though the Europeans had no problem identifying themselves as French, Germans, or Scottish, the Africans became a monolithic group recognized only for their lack of European culture.

The issue of Annang identity has been surrounded in confusion and misinformation not only among European amateur and professional ethnographers but has also at home. Who really are the Annang? Why did some writers and ethnographers give them other identities and what are the reasons for such confusion? In previous chapters, we have seen how others have made claims about the Annang and have imposed other identities on them. This chapter will provide background, history, and reasons for this confusion and will locate this apparent crisis as emanating from Western intercourse in Africa. We will also argue that the issue of identity in Africa allows for the concentration of power on some regions for the benefit of those who seek to dominate the other. Let us begin with a brief history of Western ethnography as a way to establish a background for what is to follow.

## STUDYING OTHERS AND THE PROBLEM OF MEANING

In this section, I will borrow some ideas liberally from a paper I presented at a conference at the University of Houston in Texas, "Women in the Making of the Black World in 2001." The Annang, as other groups in Africa, were made known to the Western world through the work of the missionaries and the colonialists. Stories sent home by these two groups brought first amateur ethnographers and later professional ones. A lot has been written about the beginnings of ethnography in the Western world (Denzin and Lincoln, 1994; Vidich and Lyman, 1994). Neuman (1997) traces the roots of ethnography to the reports of travelers and the stories of European travelers dating back to 1200 AD (Ette, 2001, 2010). In almost all societies, however, it is customary for the traveled to share stories of lives and living in other lands to those at home (Ette, 2010). Among the Annang, for example, those who visited other lands came back with stories and named those they visited according to their greeting patterns and responses. Thus, the Igbos were named Uneghe, perhaps as a result of the traditional greeting pattern of the group that inquires about one's well-being and family (Nneghi). The Hausas were called Sanu based on the greeting of the same name, while the Yorubas became Akusa, a corruption of the Yoruba word for thank you (Ekushe). In Western societies, there is a large body of work that narrates stories of alien cultures by missionaries to their readers in Europe and America. Waddell (1863), a Scottish missionary, wrote of strange customs among the Efiks of southeast Nigeria and pointed out the primitivity of such customs. Much has changed since the early travelers wrote and spoke about "strange customs." The techniques of ethnography have undergone changes. But the question still remains: What were the factors that affected the interpretation and meaning of what was studied? At the root of ethnography is the emphasis on meaning. As a technique of qualitative research, ethnography concerns itself with meaning (Ette, 2009).

Marcus (1994) calls ethnography cultural translation. Ethnography then becomes the translation of a participation and perception of a social scientist in a culture to an audience. The translation involves making meaning out of symbols and interactions. Before the researcher can translate, certain processes have to take place. First, there has to be perception; what is seen is internalized and then interpreted and finally reproduced in an intelligible form to others. Translation involves the internalizing of the actions and interaction; as a result, this calls into play the translator's knowledge and background. Anything short of these steps becomes transliteration, which may render the story nonsensical (cited in Ette, 2011). Translation therefore involves the recognition of cultural differences (Atkinson and Hammerly, 1994). As a rule, what we speak about and how we speak is guided by our cultural experiences.

Ethnography is therefore presented as the other story. Neuman (1997) sees ethnography as a presentation of "accounts of unfamiliar social worlds" that describes a culture from the insider's point of view. The aim is to discover cultural meanings to the people involved. This perspective from the insider's point of view is known as the *emic* perspective; when the ethnographer describes a culture from the researcher's point of view it is known as the *etic* perspective (Gladwin, 1989). The ethnographer must be careful to ask, "What is the meaning of a particular action and interaction to the people involved?" The emic category recognized that humans are purposeful beings and seek to find out what meanings are attached to actions, symbols, and interactions by the people that are being studied in a particular society. The etic category on the other hand is generalizing. It seeks to make assumptions and offer meanings based on the researcher's cultural knowledge and background. Denzin (1989) identifies two kinds of meanings in ethnography, namely surface meaning and deep meaning. The appearance and obvious action is the surface meaning, while the deep meaning is the hidden meaning. A handshake among a teenage gang, for example, may be a handshake on the surface but has a deeper meaning of communicating something else among the gang members.

Written narratives and description of lives and living in Africa by Western travelers to those back home were, according to the above understanding, not a scientific enterprise. Additionally, those who came to study and described the Africans in colonial times were not objective scientists either (Ette, 2001). Let us turn our attention now to how the West studied Africans and what guided their assumptions.

As we noted earlier, Auguste Comte, the French philosopher, offered an explanation for the differences in cultural practice between the Western Europeans and other cultures in 1830. According to Comte, the cultures of the world could be arranged to form a chain. This continuum, he wrote, could locate the stages of development from the low to the advanced. The technique for locating the evolutionary stage of a culture was by looking at its technology and other social indicators. Certain practices and objects in a culture, he said, could help individuals tell if a particular culture was at the stage of savagery, barbarism, or civilization. According to Comte, all cultures began at the same time; however, certain cultures had an arrested development and failed to progress. These cultures remained stagnant either at the level of savagery or barbarism. Thankfully, the Western European culture did not face any hindrance and moved to the stage of civilization (Ette, 2012).

This Eurocentric developmental framework resulted in the center/periphery dichotomy in early ethnography with the European cultures forming the center and all others making up the periphery. It simplified the task of studying cultures and according to Vidich and Lyman (1994) "made the work of the ethnographer much simpler, the task became that of a classifier of cultural traits in transition or arrest" (p. 28). The Western culture by this model represented the advanced and civilized stage in the evolutionary hierarchy and thus made the center, while other cultures represented the low level and constituted the periphery. The understanding of the arrested development theory presented the other cultures as a window to the primitive past. By looking at these cultures, the reasoning went, the observer could see the past in the present. Armed with this theory, early missionaries, amateur ethnographers, and even the colonial administrators who came to Africa set about to describe and interpret alien and "primitive" cultures to the civilized readers of the Western world. Hope Masterson Waddell (1863), a Presbyterian missionary with the Efiks of southeastern Nigeria, for example, wrote thus of the Efik language:

> The Efik is a simple and primitive tongue in many respects, of Semitic character. Though defective, as the unwritten language of an unlettered people might be expected to be, it has such a grammatical structure as renders it capable of great improvement. (Waddell, 1970, p. 673)

On marriage among the Efik, he continued:

> Their marriage implies no formal or binding engagements of any kind; though it is understood, of course, naturally that faithfulness and obedience are due on the wife's part, support and protection on his. The entire dependence of wives there on their husbands for all things, lay them under life bonds for their good behavior, while he remains free to act as he likes in all respect. (Waddell, 1970, p. 667)

Social researchers also followed this Comtean model and worked to find evidence for preconceived beliefs. The method of doing research about other cultures at this stage was just a matter of locating the stage of the culture on a Comtean scale. In 1911, for example, a North American Yahi Indian was captured and transferred to San Francisco where he was put on display at the university's Museum of Anthropology as an example of a primitive and wild man until his death four years and seven months later. In *Ishi in Two Worlds*, Kroeber (1961) wrote,

"Ishi was the last wild Indian in North America, a man of Stone Age culture subjected for the first time when he was past middle age to twentieth century culture" (p. 9).

What was different between European and other cultures became strange and primitive, and what was not understood had a constructed meaning to fit the Eurocentric worldview and the center/periphery thinking. What was different was considered the periphery, and European culture became the center of the universe (Ette, 2009). Historicism represented to these early ethnographers a real method for understanding non-European cultures. What happened to Ishi was not new. In 1904, Samuel Verner had put an East African Pigmy, Ota Benga, on display at the Saint Louis World's Fair in the United States as an example of a primitive person. A year later, Ota Benga was transferred to the monkey house at the Bronx Zoo (Vidich and Lyman, 1994). He later committed suicide after African American groups secured his release.

Another approach was for the ethnographers to consider non-European cultures as unspoiled and untainted. Lewis Morgan in 1877 studied the Native American population and described the society as "a stateless primitive society founded on communal property." Federich Engel (1884) was so impressed by this description that he assailed the "primitive" and "untainted" nature of the natives that was not corrupted by capitalism. Western capitalism, Engel wrote, has corrupted Western civilization. He continued:

> Naked greed has been the moving spirit of civilization from the first day of its existence to the present time, wealth, more wealth, and wealth again; wealth not of society, but of this shabby individual was its sole and determining aim. (Engel, 1978, p. 757)

This became the point of departure for Marxist ethnographers. They saw the "noble savage" in other cultures and looked for evidence of economic and social purities. There was nothing different in what the Marxist ethnographers were doing. Like others, they were busy looking for evidence to fit a preconceived notion. The non-European cultures still represented an arrested development. These cultures were still looked upon as a window to the past. In *A Profile of Primitive Culture*, Service (1958) gave a "profile of primitive cultures" from North America to Asia and laboriously pointed out the effects of the blessings of Western contact on these primitive people. Cultural practices of the other were seen as relics of ancient times. In his introduction to *Our Primitive Contemporaries*, George Murdock (1934) asked, "How does the savage actually live?" He then proceeded to answer his question in the rest of the book by showing the primitivity of the Tasmanians, the Ganda, the Crows, and other cultural groups. In his analysis of the Tasmanians, Murdock (1934) showed the simple minds and childlike instincts of this group:

> The Tasmanians lived only for the passing moment. Their wants were few and in general easily satisfied. They indulged in their simple animal pleasures without thought of the future. Thus when food was plentiful they gorged themselves and were happy, but they accumulated no stores. In bad winters consequently, they suffered severely from hunger, and were even forced at times to gnaw on Kangaroo skins. (Murdock, 1934, p. 15)

There was complicity with the colonizers. The unflattering account of the natives sought to justify the colonization of the people and presented the people studied as childlike minds who needed the benevolence of the colonialists. Davis (1933) in describing the lives of the South African industrial worker wrote:

> When not at work the native loafs about his hut or keeps up an incessant chatter with other men of similar shift hours . . . he has no desire and little encouragement to spend his off hours in either constructive recreational or other self-improvement occupation. His rather drab life flows on through the weeks of his engagement. (Davis, 1933, p. 63)

## CONFUSION OVER ANNANG IDENTITY AND THE POLITICS OF HEGEMONY

Knowledge of groups and issues of identity in Africa have been influenced by some of these old writings. Tainted by false assumptions, the early ethnographers went about assigning identities to those that they met. Old identities and claims were discarded in favor of those made up by the ethnographers, colonialists, and missionaries. The lack of recognition of identity of the Annang by some people has been seen as a problem by many observers and indigenes of Annang. A cursory look in the literature will reveal that the Annang began to lose their cultural and ethnic identity gradually while at the same time having other identities imposed on them. They assumed a hyphenated identity and name that historically had not been part of their understanding. The Annang were no longer referred to as Annang but "Annang-Ibibio" or "Efik" and by others as Igbo. These new hyphenated or nonhyphenated names conveyed a new identity. More than just a normative category, it represented their position in the Nigerian political arena. We shall return again to this issue, but for now the legitimate question to raise here is: How did this happen?

Homogenization and the denial of identities are sadly part of the postcolonial African political history and have sadly contributed to the patterns of communal conflict in the continent. It is often used as a weapon and a claim on the other for political advantage. As Young (1995) observed, homogenization has become an attempt to create "nations" by the new political elites to conform to the boundaries of what they were handed by the colonialists as new nations. Among those in southern Nigeria, homogenization has become an attempt to dominate and create an artificial "nation" by groups who seek to dominate others for political advantage. It is no longer the old boundaries created by imperialist powers of the past that is the problem. Internal politics and the creation of new political units called states in Nigeria have also forced integration of cleavages to conform to new boundaries of the new states. Military authorities and political leaders have fashioned states to fit with their vision of what the political units should be. The Yorubas of Nigeria, for example, fought to homogenize the Edos and resisted the creation of the midwest region. Among the intellectual class in newsgroups on the internet, heated arguments abound about issues of identity. Whether the homogenization of Annang is responsible for the lack of the creation of the proposed Itai State—a political unit for the Annang—is best left for history and those who would analyze the postcolonial history and ethnic relations in the country. Yet it can be argued that the new hyphenated identity of the Annang, more than simply being seen as a product of conspiracy, may be rooted in history and the work of Western amateur ethnographers who rushed to Africa to report on the lives of those they saw as primitive. The rush to homogenize new political boundaries seeks to convey political advantages to those who dominate the political arena. Though the current confusion over the Annang identity has something to do with the internal politics in Nigeria, it has its genesis in the story of those who knew very little about the people that they were writing about. It is however now maintained by the new political class. The confusion over Annang identity was created by the Western writers who saw all Africans as savages and were looking at locating the primitive life of those they saw on the Comtean scale as was noted earlier.

Let us turn our attention to a review of the work of the early "ethnographers" and see how they saw the Annang. We will begin first with the reports of the Christian missionaries, then the colonial agents, and finally reports of travelers and scientists. The aim is to discover how each contributed to or took away from correctly identifying the Annang group. We will end the section by comparing the early reports with contemporary ideas and identification of the Annang among modern ethnographers and writers.

## MISSIONARY REPORTS

As noted earlier in this book, Western contact with those ethnic groups outside the coastal areas in what is today Nigeria is very recent. Though the Presbyterian missionaries arrived in Calabar in the middle of the nineteenth century, contact with those in the hinterland were limited because of restrictions placed on the Europeans by Efik chiefs and their agents. Additionally, the difficulty of traveling outside of Calabar with limited means of transportation was enormous. The early missionaries therefore restricted their activities to Calabar and the creeks around it. The little that the missionaries knew about groups other than the Efiks came from the European merchants and ship workers who did not venture far from their ships for safety reasons. Daryll (1956) described the sea merchants as "fleeting visitors." Thus, the missionaries, like other Europeans as we shall see later, accepted stereotypical descriptions of those they did not know and because of racism saw all Africans in the area as feeble minded. The region therefore consisting of the Annang and Ibibio lands was seen in the words of the mission historian Marwick (1897) as "the region . . . of the darkness and shadow of death" and their inhabitants "not merely a band of unfortunates, but a company of criminals—an army of rebels of mutineers" (p. 367). Given such understanding, the missionaries on the coast in Calabar focused their attention on imparting the creeds of the Christian religion, which they saw as the only hope of saving the Africans. Everything else had to contribute to this goal. Writing about the mission school in Calabar, for example, Reverend Hope Waddell wrote in his memoir:

> We had in our hands as it were the forming of future generations. Commerce had done nothing and could do nothing for the moral and spiritual improvement of that ignorant and brutish people. Christian truth alone, with God's blessing could change them in that respect, and on that change every other of any value depended. (Waddell, 1970 p. 348)

Change, meaning the acculturation of the Africans, was the ultimate goal in the missionary enterprise. Given such a goal, the correct identification and the description of the people were not necessary. To the early missionaries, the Africans were simply "ignorant and brutish people." Yet the Calabar area, Waddell observed, consisted of "small republics, each with its own chiefs and councils" (Waddell, 1970, p. 314).

Why did the early missionaries make the mistake of confusing the ethnic groups that they met? Given the misinformation that existed at the time, they knew very little about those outside of Calabar. The expansion of the missionary enterprise to Itu and the spread of colonialism were to change all that. Yet the imperfect knowledge of customs, history, and language made the proper identification of the people difficult. Racism presented a barrier that was difficult to cross between the indigenes and the European missionaries. The fear of becoming ill and the threat posed by malaria necessitated frequent furloughs in Europe, which took the missionary away for long periods at a time. Many of the missionaries who became ill also returned to Europe for extended periods of time. Therefore, though a particular missionary could claim years in the African field, the actual time spent in the field was considerably less. Some of the interpreters for the Europeans were outsiders who either harbored old prejudices or did not know enough to translate accurately to the missionaries. It would take further contact by other Europeans living among the Annang to recognize that the Annang were a separate group. Finally, the biographers of the missionaries who wrote after the deaths of those who served in the field assumed that the areas that they served were homogenous, for the most part; however, the confusion of who the Annang were stemmed from ignorance.

Nowhere else was this ignorance as apparent as in the letters that Mary Slessor wrote to her friend, the colonial officer Mr. Partridge. Beginning in the early part of the 1900s, personal letters written to Mr. Partridge were addressed to him at Ikot Okpene, Ibibio, and at other times the letter simply carried the address of Ikot Okpene, Old Calabar (Letters to Mr. Partridge). Thus, the Annang were either Ibibio or Efiks without a clear understanding of who they really were. Those who read such letters had a choice of calling the Annang either Ibibio or Efik. It is not a surprise, therefore, that the Slessor biographer, Livingstone (1916), identified Ikot Ekpene as Ibibio territory at some points and at others as part of the Igbo territory of Arochukwu.

Reverend Groves who lived in Ikot Ekpene among the Annang between 1915 and 1932, on the other hand, and who learned to speak the Annang language in his papers correctly identified the people he lived with as Annang, whereas those who lived in Ibibio land wrote back home to Europe identifying the Annang as either Efik, Ibibio, or Igbo. Reverend Groves and those who spoke to Annang elders did not make the mistake that others who lived outside Annangland did.

## REPORTS OF COLONIAL AGENTS AND TRAVELERS

The Scottish missionaries arrived in Calabar more than four hundred years after the Dutch discovered that they could buy articles of trade and slaves that could be sold in Europe. As Talbot (1926) observed, Calabar was not shown on Spanish and Portuguese maps of the fifteenth and sixteenth centuries but only on those used by Dutch merchants in the sixteenth century. When the English finally arrived and had become the colonial masters in the middle of the nineteenth century, the stories that their agents and travelers sent back to Europe were written for the entertainment and information of their European readers, essentially telling tales of the bizarre and "primitive."

Though the colonial administration collected and kept information on the areas that they administered, the purpose for which such information was collected was not for scientific and empirical reasons. Such information was for ease of administration and for the safety of the colonial state that had nothing to do with a correct description and categorizing of the people. Under the prevailing racist views, the groups were all seen as homogenous, so much so that when Messenger (1957) attempted a scientific ethnographic study of the Annang area, he warned against the use of earlier European reports. In the first scientific study of the Annang, Messenger (1957) found that "the Europeans living in the (Annang) area had a superficial knowledge of the indigenous people" (p. iii). Yet the reports of these colonial agents and European travelers with their minimal knowledge of the Annang have been used by many writers to discuss authoritatively about the Annang, which some have variously referred to as Ibibio, Efik, or Igbos.

Although several colonial agents wrote about the people they met in southern Nigeria, two writers have had tremendous impact on how later generation of writers have defined those who live in southern Nigeria and subsequently the identity given to the indigenes of the area including the Annang. The first is M. D. W. Jeffreys and the other is F. N. Ashley. Both of these men came to Ikot Ekpene as district officers after World War I and spent less than ten years in the area. Though they worked as colonial agents and interacted through Efik and Igbo interpreters, they managed to collect information to share with others at home. M. D. W. Jeffreys would later publish two books from his notes, *Old Calabar* and *Notes on Ibibio Language*. He returned to his native South Africa and devoted his time to the study of "primitive people," contributing monographs and letters to journals interested in publishing materials that supported Darwinian ideas. F. N. Ashley also wrote an unpublished monograph titled *On Ikot Ekpene*. Messenger (1957) reported that when he tried to use these writings in his study of the Annang he found them unreliable. Yet these individuals would later use information collected during their years as colonial officers as materials for scholarly papers, thereby passing on wrong information and polluting scholarship about the Annang. Jeffreys and Ashley like other colonial agents of the time dealt on stereotypes and stories handed down to them that had no relevance to the Annang. They too could not differentiate between the Annang, the Efiks, the Ibibios, and the Igbos.

Besides Ashley and Jeffreys, Talbot (1915) and her husband Talbot (1923) are the two most quoted authorities on those who live in southern Nigeria. Talbot served as a colonial agent following the opening of the interior in 1901 (Messenger, 1957). He and his wife were interested in the "primitive" culture that they saw and set out to document it. On their return to Europe, Mr. Talbot published *Life in Southern Nigeria* in 1923. This was followed by what are considered the authoritative sources of information on the region: his two volumes of *The People of Southern Nigeria* in 1926. His wife documented the lives of the women she saw in the area in her book *Woman's Mysteries of a Primitive People* (1915). The problem with these volumes as Messenger found out when he tried to use the Talbots' as a source was that "much of the information they (The Talbots) collected is of little use for an understanding of Annang culture" (Messenger, 1957, p. v). They wrote about the Annang neighbors in Obudu and Eket and generalized what they found to the Annang. Because they had no scientific training in ethnography, what they collected and described had very little to do with the Annang. Talbot (1915) in a pure Comtean method divided the groups that she met in Obudu, Eket, Calabar, and Ibibioland into two groups of cultures, one in transition and the other in a state of arrest. The Talbots never lived in Annang. Thus, according to their observation, the Efiks were more civilized and the Ibibio were the ones in a state of arrest. She opined in her book, "Saving the more civilised Efiks, it is indisputable that the Ibibios occupy a low rung on the ladder of culture" (Talbot, 1915, p. 4). Thus, all who lived outside of Calabar and outside of Eket where the Talbots were or those considered "uncivilized" automatically became either Ibibio or Igbo. This classification would be later adopted by others to define the Annang.

## THE SOCIAL SCIENTISTS' REPORTS

Until 1966, many anthropologists did not know about the Annang and until then the Annang language was not known by linguists. Using the wrong information supplied by travelers and colonial agents, many in the scientific and academic community either assumed that the Annang were Ibibios, Efiks, or Igbos as noted earlier. The first scientific study of the group was done by Messenger (1957), who as earlier pointed out discovered that past descriptions of the group were wrong. Messenger set out by immersing himself in the community. He utilized the observation method and participated in cultural activities including joining secret societies. He further discovered that interviewing tended to reveal the ideal instead of the real behavior and meaning. Moreover, he discovered that the Annang had "considerable deviations" from what former travelers and amateur ethnographers described. In a doctoral dissertation presented to Northwest University in Evansville, Illinois, in the United States in 1957, Dr. Messenger for the first time undertook a scientific study of the Annang group.

However, the misidentification of the Annang has persisted and follows a predicted course since the Annang were first wrongly classified by amateur ethnographers. Recent writers have continued to follow these old but wrong descriptions giving different identities to them.

## IMPLICATION FOR INDIVIDUAL IDENTITY

This analysis is more than just an intellectual exercise and perhaps could form a lesson in how not to make generalizations, but for those who are defined by these normative categories, the description carries real-life implications regarding their identities and position in present day Nigeria. The Annang have been defined and identified without their knowledge and input. Ekanem (2002) related a story of writing for his undergraduate school magazine and in that article referred to himself as Efik, a term applied to all those who lived in southeast Nigeria by the British since the introduction of Efik as a language of instruction in 1933. It took his adviser reading that article to correct the young Annang man that he was not an Efik but Annang. That story has been repeated several times and in numerous situations where individuals erroneously assume other identities. This story illustrates the problem facing the Annang and the damage imposed by Western amateur anthropologists and political classification based on the goal of hegemony.

If the Annang identity was shaped by politics and the imperfect knowledge of Westerners in the pre-independence period, certainly the postindependence period when Africans had the opportunity to reshape and remake their identity would be different. The postindependence period would, however, bring a new era in the struggle for the Annang identity, and this will form the subject of the next chapter.

*Chapter Ten*

# Postindependence and Civil War

Falola (1998) has described Nigeria "as many nations within one" (p. 45). To understand the issues of ethnicity and ethnic conflict in the country, therefore, one must have a simple knowledge of Nigeria's history. Nigeria became independent from Great Britain in 1960. Following independence, the country saw a brief period of civil rule until 1966, when a group of Igbo military officers overthrew the parliamentary system of government led by the late Prime Minister Tafawa Balewa. In the confusion that followed the coup, General Aguyi Ironsi assumed power and abolished the federal structure. He also introduced a unitary system for governing the country. The police force was centralized, the constitution suspended, and all ethnic associations were also banned. The Ibibio State Union, discussed previously in this book, became a casualty of the ban. A series of retaliatory killings by the mainly Hausa officers resulted in the assassination of General Ironsi who was an Igbo. Gowon, a northerner, became the new military ruler (Forsyth, 1969). Though he divided the former four regions into twelve states as a way of minimizing the effect of ethnicity and regionalism, the country continued to be governed as a unitary state and all decisions affecting the units were made at the center in an effort to minimize and deemphasize ethnicity. The eastern section of the country under the leadership of Colonel Odumegwu Ojukwu broke away and declared itself the Republic of Biafra. A civil war that followed resulted in the deaths of many people. Ethnicity in Nigeria and indeed Africa, as previously noted, has enormous implications for security and life.

Several Annang individuals went to work for the state and federal civil service following independence. Others held elective posts in the capital. In the killings of the southerners in 1966, many were forced to return and sought shelter in their native villages. When the Nigerian army attacked the Annang area, they brought a list of names along and went through the homes of those whose names were on the list and took them away. No figures exist on the number of people killed during the Nigerian civil war that raged from 1967 to 1970, but the Annang suffered disproportionately. Those who served in the Eastern House of Assembly, the regional executives, the federal legislature, and the federal executives left their posts to escape the killings in the north. Back in the east, as the war raged, these leaders became sitting targets for those who supported other political parties. Because most of the Annang were supporters of the Igbo-led NCNC before the war, they were seen as enemies by members of the other parties and were systematically exterminated. Some corrupt Nigerian army officers colluded with the Annang enemies and went from house to house picking up these Annang leaders. Family members were told that the commanding officer needed them to answer some questions or help with projects. Taken from their homes, they were never heard from again; some articles of clothing were sometimes found on the street and became a part of the evidence that they were murdered.

In this chapter, we attempt to argue that though there is a shared relatedness associated with ethnicity among Nigerians, the idea has chiefly been exploited by the elites when it suited them and has been used as an instrument of destabilization. We further seek to argue that such difference was also used by the colonialists to advance the interest of the crown in Nigeria.

Etounga-Manguelle (2000) related a story of an unnamed African government minister who in remarks at an event was carried away and so he said, "When we gained power, the country was at the edge of an abyss: since, we have taken a great step forward" (p. 66). This minister was stating the obvious without realizing it. Between World War II and the close of the last century, countries in the African continent have thrown away the yoke of colonialism; despite this development, the dividends of democracy are seldom noticed in the continent. Other societies and countries have grown and developed, but Africa has remained in the words of Roe (1999) the "except-for" continent. As countries in other regions enjoyed the boom of the 1990s, African countries lagged behind. The history of the continent and events have often been framed either as a vilification of the colonialists and missionaries on one hand or as the idealization of the past by Afrocentric intellectuals on the other. Yet very few examine closely the contribution and failure of the political and intellectual elites in African development or backwardness. We have seen in previous chapters the contribution of the Western missionaries, scientists, and colonialists in issues surrounding identities and group relations in southern Nigeria. When colonialism ended, however, the African elites and those who were closer to the colonialists took up leadership positions in the postcolony. Like the missionaries, the African religious leaders played supporting roles to the indigenous leaders just like the missionaries helped the colonialists. This chapter will explore the role of the African elites in shaping group relations and how this affected the Annang. The chapter will argue that rather than seek to unite the different groups under the new flag, the new elites in Nigeria exploited ethnic differences for their selfish ends and in the process diminished the gains of independence and democracy.

Ethnicity has been politicize in Africa and we are faced with what Ake (1992) called political ethnicity, defining it as the "politicization and transformation of ethnic exclusivity into major political cleavages" (p. 2). Ake traces the history of political ethnicity in Nigeria with the advent of colonialism. Indirect rule became necessary because the British government was not willing to commit resources to run the colonies. Reliance on the traditional structures or in the case of Annang the manufacture of structures to achieve the colonial aims politicized ethnic relations and created competition between groups. Those closer to the colonialists and missionaries were rewarded with Western education and such status created an advantage. The postcolonial period was not different. Advantages and numerical strength led to more competition and the native politicians exploited ethnicity for selfish gains. Following independence, the African states became repressive and individuals turned to ethnic groups as centers of resistance (Ake, 1992). For the Annang, aligning with the Igbos and choosing to remain with the Azikiwe-led NCNC led to Annang leaders paying a high price during the civil war.

## FEDERAL CHARACTER AND THE POLITICS OF PLUNDER

Across Africa, ethnicity has been used as a tool of exploitation to conceal corruption by the political class. It has further become an instrument of building solidarity across social class lines. Political discourse is often framed as the malevolence of the other who wishes other groups no good. Millions have been made to believe that a position of government for a member of the group benefits all from the group. In Nigeria, the colonial idea that civil service is an end in itself continues to be the focal point and is reflected in the language of the 1999 Nigerian Constitution. Thus, the Federal Character Commission in the Nigerian 1999 Constitution is taxed with the responsibility to

> promote, monitor and enforce compliance with the principles of proportional sharing of all bureaucratic, economic, media and political posts at all levels of government. (Sec. 153 [8] [1]b)

Rather than promote nondiscrimination, common citizenship, and equal justice as a bill of rights, the nation has managed to codified ethnicity. The euphemism and what has come to be known as "federal character" is a quota system that had its origin in the 1979 Constitution (Eke and Osaghae, 1989). The federal character principle mandates the sharing of positions and benefits according to the ethnolinguistic and religious variables of the country in the assumption that what is given to one individual benefits the group. Yet the reality is that those who are often the beneficiaries of such positions are those with the credentials that allow them to get their foot in the door. Such positions hardly benefit the poor and those without education. Because ethnic and religious cleavages converge in Nigeria, the situation becomes the more complicated and often ethnic tensions take on religious tones as well in the north-south geographical divide (Obianyo, 2008). However, among the Annang as was noted earlier, the forced conversion of the group to Christianity and the linkage that existed between the missionaries and the educational institution resulted in the elite class, who were educated in Christian schools, becoming Christians and those without education practicing the traditional religion. Recently, however, the introduction of the American conservative Christian movement with its emphasis on personal sanctification has generated what Pat Buchanan, the American conservative commentator, called the culture war. The young educated urban dwellers that join these traditional "nondenominational churches" often pastored by popular preachers look down on the indigenous culture and look at specific cultural activities as sinful. Popular indigenous festivals have been abandoned by the educated class and even traditional names given to children no longer find currency. In what Mbembe (2001) calls the "aesthetics of vulgarity," new ideas and practices are invented that generate new political adulterated consciousness and confusion.

In Akwa Ibom State where the Annang live, one such idea was what was referred to as the "consensus candidate" in 2008. Victor Attah, having served two terms as governor of Akwa Ibom State and unable to serve another term because of the term limit imposed by the Nigerian Constitution, announced that a governorship candidate from Annang should be supported by his party, the People Democratic Party or the PDP. What Mr. Attah failed to disclose was that Mr. Ekarika, his son-in-law who is an Annang man, was interested in running for the office of governor. In the party primaries, Mr. Godswill Akpabio, another Annang man, appeared to be getting more support and so in the confusion that ensued, some called for the disqualification of both Mr. Akpabio and Mr. Ekarika and the suspension of further voting in favor of "a consensus candidate" that would be acceptable to the opposing sides. The idea of a consensus candidate was given as a solution to end the impasse between groups supporting the former governor, Victor Attah, and those supporting the candidacy of Godswill Akpabio. Though supporters of the latter won, the vulgarity of an undemocratic idea presented as a compromise raises the question about the place and understanding of democracy. It further demonstrates, as Mbembe rightly pointed out, the nature of subordination and domination of the present Annang society by the political elite. They are willing and ready to suspend the tenets and practices of democracy when it does not suit certain designs and goals. How then did it get to this point?

## THE NIGERIAN CIVIL WAR AND ITS CAUSES

To understand the politics affecting the Annang in the postcolonial era is to return to the group experience in the Nigerian civil war that raged between 1967 and 1970. The analysis also requires a look at the post–civil war experience of the Annang as well as the economic and social conditions before and following the Nigeria civil war. To understand the issue of ethnicity and ethnic conflict in Nigeria, one must have a simple knowledge of Nigeria's history.

The British colonialists preferred the Muslims and saw them as more civilized and more intelligent than the southerners that they saw as uncivilized and unintelligent (Falola, 1998). It is, however, ironic that while the Western missionaries were building schools to impart Western education and Christian religion in the south, their compatriots in the colonial office were protecting the interests of Islam in the north. The British colonialists bought into the ethnocentrism of the northern elites who saw their southern neighbors as infidels and worse, as uncivilized. In opposing the amalgamation of the north and south, Tafawa Balewa, who would later become prime minister, wass quoted as saying:

> We do not want, Sir, our Southern neighbors to interfere in our development. . . . I should like to make it clear to you that if the British quitted Nigeria now at this stage the Northern people would continue their interrupted conquest to the sea. (Quoted in Forsyth, 1969, p. 18)

The Muslims did find sympathetic ears from the British, who made every effort not to challenge them (the Muslims) provided they did not interfere with their colonial goals. The north opposed the amalgamation of the south and the north with ethnocentric reasons and the governor, Sir Authur Richards, went along with that and agreed with the conditions the north gave, namely separate regional government with the north having a majority in the legislature and the enshrinement of separate development in the new constitution. These conditions that Forsyth called the "seeds of regionalism" resulted in what he further termed "the attempted marriage of irreconcilables" (1969).

O'Connell (1969) provided three main reasons for the cause of the civil war, namely colonial set up, unrealistic expectations about independence and education, and the lack of able leadership. He agreed with Forsyth that the issue of the north having a larger size and more representation given them in Richard's Constitution than the south was to be blamed. He further observed that the people were led to believe that their lives would change for the better following independence; yet such expectation was unrealistic given the lack of able leadership and the enormous economic challenge facing the country after independence. Additionally, the people had come to believe that Western education changed lives and provide big dividends, yet such expectations were also unrealistic because those who were educated soon discovered that opportunities were limited. Given these conditions, he maintained, political instability arose and this led to the civil war.

The civil war did affect the Annang more than other groups in eastern Nigeria. Those who lived in the northern part of the country lost their lives and all who escaped lost their properties and were left with nothing. There was no compensation and no government help in resettling the victims. Professor Aluko (1969) put the estimate of the returnees from the northern part of the country to the east at 1.6 million. Of these numbers, 300,000 or 20 percent were children. Those who returned disabled constituted 0.6 percent or 10,000 people, while 1 percent or 15,000 were elderly and could not work. Only 15 percent of the displaced persons were married (Aluko, 1969). Unfortunately, no figures exist specifically about the number of Annang who were displaced and had to return to their villages as they were all counted as Igbos by international aid groups and by the Nigerian intellectual elites in the Aluko Report. Following the massacres of October 1966 and the displacement of southerners from the north to the south, the civil war began on July 6, 1967. The period between the massacre in the north and the beginning of the civil war may be characterized as the period of propaganda. School children were taught war songs and how to stay safe in the event of attack. Colonel Odumegwo Ojukwu, the leader of the rebellion, declared that the eastern region was now an independent nation to be known and called Biafra. Reports of the progress of the war spread through news broadcasts. Colonel Ojukwu had released his friend, a Yoruba man, named Victor Banjo from jail in Enugu and had given him the rank of brigadier in the Biafran Army (Forsyth, 1969). It was this trusted friend that Ojukwu gave the responsibility to handle the war in the west. Despite limited arms, the Biafran soldiers moved swiftly and took the whole midwestern region and moved as far as Ore just a few miles from the then capital, Lagos. Gowon planned to flee the country and abandoned the war when most of his soldiers were killed and he realized that it was a matter of time before the Biafran Army took Lagos. But for the intervention and advice of the British and the Americans, Forsyth maintained, he would have fled. With a promise of arms and aid, the British and Americans urged him to stay and fight. The Nigerian leader engaged then in massive recruitments, enlisting anyone strong enough to join the army. School dropouts, jobless individuals, and prison inmates became soldiers and were given guns after just a week's training (Forsyth, 1969).

Perhaps the biggest setback that prevented the march of the Biafran Army into Lagos as expected was the betrayal of Victor Banjo, the once-trusted friend of the Biafran leader who commanded the western front. Unknown to the Biafran leader, Brigadier Banjo had arranged to stop the march into Lagos. He further wanted to recruit Yoruba leaders, assassinate Ojukwu, stopped the Biafran rebellion, and gain himself the top spot as the leader of Nigeria. While feeding false information to Ojukwu on the lack of progress at the war front, he was secretly plotting against Biafra. On September 12, 1967, Banjo gave orders and withdrew his troops from Benin and the midwest "without firing a single shot" (Forsyth, 1969, p. 112). It took the Nigerian soldiers until September 21 to move into the vacuum created by the withdrawal. The fortunes of Biafra were thus reversed and the Nigerian troops, with arms from America and Great Britain, pushed the Biafran troops now with earnest further south.

## THE KWASHIORKOR SCOURGE

It is difficult to write about the Annang experience in the Nigerian civil war without mentioning the kwashiorkor epidemic that killed thousands of men, women, and children more than the bullets. The Nigerian government on the advice of its foreign military backers used blockades and starvation as tactics of war. Food importation was not allowed into the Biafra territory and farming in a war zone was not an option in the constant shrinking war-ravaged territory and therefore starvation and the kwashiorkor disease led many to an early grave. The disease also known as edematous malnutrition is brought about by a lack of protein in the diet and is seen in areas in which there is famine, political unrest, and individuals are not able to eat properly. It is characterized by changes in hair and skin color and retention of water in the extremities and belly. Other symptoms include the wasting away of skin and bone, lethargy, and finally death. The cascades of infections due to the damaged immune system, as well as the inability to grow and gain weight, are extremely disastrous to young children. This is what those in the Annang area went through. Despite attempts and appeals from churches, aid groups, and journalists, the Nigerian government refused to lift the blockades and all proposals were passed through the British government that evaluated them according to whether it conveyed a military advantage to the Nigerian military (Forsyth, 1969). As a result, the death went on unabated. Salt was difficult to come by and protein was not a part of the diet if food could be found at all. Starvation as a weapon of war was seen as a legitimate tactic of war, and the Nigerian military did not make a secret of it. Dead bodies from the disease littered the streets of major towns as children orphaned by the war fell and died. Those who survived saw stunted growth.

## THE WAR IN ANNANGLAND

The Annang became particularly affected when the war turned toward the city of Calabar. Soon Calabar fell to the national troops and they advanced north toward an old trading town called Itu. Heavy bombardments and shelling could be heard especially at night in the Annang town of Ikot Ekpene. Soon the war drew closer. On March 30, 1968, federal troops entered Ikot Ekpene Township (Adeolu, 2017). With just a few short weeks of training and some released from prisons in a desperate bid to repel the Biafran soldiers, the Nigerian soldiers who arrived in Ikot Ekpene were a nondisciplined bunch. They confiscated livestock and women were forcibly taken. Life was insecure and, as we noted earlier, Annang leaders were removed and slaughtered like animals. Civilians were shot and killed for real or imagined crimes and often accused of colluding with the Biafrans, though no evidence existed. Uko Akpan, the Annang popular singer, told a story of returning from market where he had gone to buy cocoyam during the war. He was caught on his return and accused of supplying food to the Biafran soldiers and was almost killed. Others were not so lucky and were often asked to dig their graves often beside the road before they were shot and killed. Passers-by were then forced to cover the open graves of strangers they never met. Women waited at home in vain for husbands and sons that would never return, and children hoped against hope that their parents would one day return. Thus, the Annang were systematically eliminated.

By April, Biafra had retaken the town of Ikot Ekpene and the residents fled to the Ibibio territory where they encountered roadblocks. Most of these were manned by vigilante groups with past grudges who accused the Annang of supporting the Biafra cause. The men were mostly led away and slaughtered and were never seen again. No one knows how many died this way, but it is estimated that more than ten thousand were killed simply because of who they were. The stereotype that the Annang individual always has a machete was used to eliminate mostly men, and women became widows and children were orphaned. At Uyo, with no refugee camp and no rehabilitation or welfare services, life was hard for the survivors, many grieving the losses of family members. The twenty-mile walk through some of the densest forest took a toll on the young and the aged. Those who escaped the bullet at home died at the hands of the vigilante murderous gang, and those who were lucky enough to escape from there died of hunger and exposure to the elements at Uyo.

In this chapter, we have attempted to give a narrative of the Nigerian civil war experience of the Annang. The view of the war through the global and national lens to the specific angle of the Annangs has been explored. The issues of ethnicity and its effects on the war have been explored. We have argued that the experience of the civil war changed the Annang society. Ikot Ekpene, the cultural and political capital of the Annangs, which was the site of the British experiment in self-governance in 1957 following the massacre of its citizens, became a shell of its old self. Nigeria murdered its own citizens, and the treatment of individuals became worse than they experienced during British colonialism. The events of the civil war, as shown, revealed that though the British granted independence to Nigeria in 1960, they did not actually leave and still meddled in Nigeria's internal affairs a few short years later. Yet it was the Nigerian military and political elites that presided over the pogrom. It was the Annang neighbors who provided a list to the military of who should be eliminated. In the next chapter, we will examine some current pressing issues and attempt to provide some suggestions in moving forward.

*Chapter Eleven*

# The Future

As already noted, the Annang live in the southeast section of Nigeria in what is now called Akwa Ibom State with the Igbos to the west and the Ibibios in the east. Prior to British colonialism, the group had between fifteen to twenty clans, with each clan headed by a leader known as Akuku (Messenger, 1957). Each clan had a food taboo and all members of the clan strictly adhered to such taboo. Thus, it is possible even today to recognize and trace the migration patterns of the Annang based on the food taboo of each clan because individual members maintained such taboos despite separation from the group of origin. The British colonial policy forced the unification of several clans and significantly weakened the office of the Akuku (Messenger, 1957). The elites in the postcolony have continued this vulgarity not to improve society, but to enable plunder and dominance of their group over the others. As Forsyth (1969) again reminded us, "In Africa . . . political power means success and prosperity, not only for the man who holds it, but for his family" (p. 23). National policies have thus become a series of practices of the vulgar loaded with impunity once power is obtained. Power is sought by any means necessary and those who stand in the way are certain to become casualties of the naked ambition. In this chapter, we shall examine current practices and attempt to make suggestions for the future. Through the story of the Annang, we shall attempt an examination of the future of minority groups in Nigeria. Furthermore, the chapter will proffer some suggestions as to how to improve the political and ethnic relation in the country.

## CLASS STRUGGLE AND POLICY

Though we have already alluded to the economic and social conditions of the people before the 1950s, it is pertinent to recall the remarks of Sir Bernard Bourdillon before the presentation of Richard's Constitution in 1954. In a paper presentation, Sir Bourdillon, the governor general of Nigeria, noted that there were two classes of people in Nigeria, each fighting for its own interest. First, there was the professional salaried and trading class; second was the peasant class who often were the primary producers. The last group was often overlooked by the salaried educated class (quoted in Akpan, 1967). As noted earlier, the educated and salaried class went "to the extent of leading organized opposition against the chiefs" (p. 21). To this day, the Akwa Ibom State government still has the Ministry of Local Government and Chieftaincy Affairs. The chiefs are treated as leaders of the peasant class at the local level and some are appointed by the state as the colonialist did. The "Paramount Ruler" draws a salary from the state and is expected to handle minor disputes outside the official judicial system. Thus, the Nigerian elites still maintain two parallel governments just as the colonialists did during indirect rule a century earlier. The states in Nigeria have increasingly been involved in the selection of the traditional rulers and have followed the colonial method. Traditional inheritance of the office or method of selection has been abandoned in favor of one demanded by whoever has political power and often tainted by corruption. In Calabar, for example, two traditional chieftaincy positions were rearranged and fused into one. In Yobe State, four traditional positions were made into thirteen (*This Day*, 2002). Not only are new positions created, but as we noted earlier, groups are pitted against each other through the machination of the political elites just as the colonialists did through what Segal and Doornbos (1976) called the Ankole Pattern as we saw earlier. The political elites have also invented new identities just as the colonialists did. This reformulation of identities has often come either because of political patronage or for the security of the political power of the rulers. While the colonialists used the Ankole Pattern for security and punitive purposes, the Nigerian political elites have used it for selfish gains and the dilution of power of groups and for dominance. A few examples will suffice here. In 1991, former general Ibrahim Babaginda created nine more states in Nigeria and used the process to either dilute the power of some groups or give others an advantage without any consideration of history or tradition. Akwa Ibom State was carved out of the former Cross-River State and Uyo was chosen as the administrative capital of the new state with no consideration that Ikot Ekpene was the oldest town, had a rich history as the first center in the experiment in local government, as well as being the cultural capital of the Annang and Ibibio as Nair (1972) noted. In the same way, Damataru was chosen over Potiskum as the new Yobe State capital despite history and the population of the latter. In Osun State, he preferred Osogbo and neglected Ife and in Delta State the former general chose Asaba rather than Warri.

Returning to the power and reason behind the power of the educated and political class, it is important to recall that the colonialists brought the English language and made fluency in the speaking and writing of the language a requirement for navigating the colonial system. Those who were able to speak and write this new language that was only taught in schools gained an advantage and were able to know what was happening within the colonial political system. Additionally, education during the colonial period bore racists and evolutionary ideas that saw the African as belonging to the primitive past, while the European culture was seen as advanced. Most schools in the colony were also organized and taught by church missionaries who sought to evangelize the natives. Education was therefore part of the civilizing mission of the natives. Hope Waddell noted in his memoir that his focus was on the young as the future. The indigenous practices, to the missionaries, became the work of the devil and European ideas and culture were portrayed as civilized, new, and Christian.

The disdain for the indigenous culture by the educated elite continued for more than fifty years afterward. In a World Bank Report on Structural Transformation and Rural Change in 2012, Nigeria still had a substantial percentage of its population that was referred to as peasant households, mostly rural and mostly poor (Losch, Fregun-Gresh, and White, 2012). What has sustained and kept the dichotomy alive has been the educational system. More than fifty years after independence, the Nigerian educated and political class that Akpan (1967) called "expatriate natives" have done little beyond lip service to change the educational curriculum. Rather than seek to change the national economic and cultural situation inherited from the colonialists, the elite has sought to use their position to dominate cultural minorities. As Freire (1970) reminded us,

> There is no such thing as a neutral educational process. Education either functions as an instrument which is used to facilitate the integration of the younger generation into the logic of the present system and bring about conformity to it, or it becomes the practice of freedom, the means by which men and women deal critically and creatively with reality and discover how to participate in the transformation of their world. (Freire, 1970 p. 15)

Using this as a starting point, and accepting the inherent logic, one rightly concludes that the "banking educational system," as Freire calls it, is at the root of the enduring maintenance of the classes in the Nigerian society in which the

Annang share. Groups with political power have seen education as a means of dominance and access of total control of the economic and political process.

## LANGUAGE AS AN INSTRUMENT OF CONTROL

What Freire (1970) wrote about concerning the lack of the neutrality in the educational process rings true in Nigeria, where the goal of education has been for the majority to exert dominance in politics through the educational process. As mentioned earlier in this book, the introduction of Efik as the language of instruction in 1933 in what was called the Calabar Province by the colonialists using the work of the Christian missionaries was not well received by the larger Ibibio group as we saw earlier. Yet in 1987, when General Babangida created Akwa Ibom State out of the former Cross-River State, the Ibibo group quickly introduced their language into the schools' curriculum throughout Annangland, though the only available texts for the teaching of the language were a series of comprehension exercises for the first four years of primary schools. It did not matter that Efik formerly introduced in schools in 1933 had extensive literature including the Holy Bible that was later translated in 1948. In fact, the Efiks themselves emigrated from Ibibioland. As we have pointed out earlier, the Ibibio State Union resented the teaching of Efik to their children. The local college also quickly began offering a new program they called Efik/Ibibio in order to produce teachers for the schools. In a statement at a conference in the state in 2018, Akwa Ibom State Commissioner for Information and Strategy Charles Udoh gave justification for the imposition of Ibibio language in Akwa Ibom State. Among his reasons were: (1) All in the state have the same destiny; (2) The introduction of a single speech pattern will bring peace, love, oneness, and harmony; and (3) Allowing groups to hold on to their language will result in "a chaotic mixture" (*Pioneer Newsonline*, 2018). Hegemonic cultural attitudes that establish the values and norms of a society are a tried and true tactic of dominance for cultural majorities. The values of the minorities, including language and religion, are often seen as not important enough to be respected and protected. Yet such violation of cultural identities has been at the root of destabilization in many societies. As we noted earlier, the claims of cultural minorities are also often dismissed. The culture and language of the other is often dismissed by a wave of the hand and certain commonalities are shown as not making them distinct. Politicians exploit fear and require reorientation in order to enjoy the rights of citizenship and prove loyalty from the minority. This is often done using the school system, which becomes the tool of sharpened identity and the arena for the gospel of hegemony. What is happening to the Annang is not different from the colonial effort that forced the learning of English on everyone, giving those who spoke English access to power. English then became the language of prestige and the language of influence. Today, the political elite want the same status for their tongue. Language acquisition becomes the ticket to entry into the political process. Unfortunately, in the effort to dominate the other, claims are made about ownership of the land or justification is made on the basis of population.

It is through this prism that the language education policies in the state where the Annang live become troublesome. The information commissioner quoted earlier used hegemony and made a sweeping claim that the Annang tongue could be dismissed as inconsequential. In fact he specifically described other tongues in the state as "a chaotic mixture." As the group resisting the language policy in the state wrote:

> It is an act of injustice to force everyone to learn one speech pattern and abandon theirs. Such action speeds up the extinction of what is not studied and codified. Teaching a language in school is not just a harmless exercise; when children learn the language of others, we are conferring influence and prestige on the language of instruction and rendering their native tongue as the language of peasants and beggars. It is the reason children refuse to speak their native language in polite company to show learning. In the end, the language of education is the language of influence and prestige. It conveys dominance and influence to the original speakers. (Letter to Commissioner Udoh, 2018)

## SUGGESTION FOR THE FUTURE

Ethnic relations and harmony are not a luxurious academic exercise but have real-life consequence with effects on capital and investment in a globalized world. In order for Nigeria to develop and thrive, ethnic conflict must be minimized and if possible eliminated; Nigerians should be made to see themselves as a diverse people who share the same country. Investors now increasingly are consulting a guide known as the International Country Risk Guide (ICRG) and looking at the ratings of individual countries before investing. The ICRG is twenty-two variables in three subcategories that tell investors if a particular country is safe to do business with (Losch, Freguine-Gresh, and White, 2012). The political risk component in this guide includes an assessment about the degree of tensions between different ethnic and racial groups in the country. It is therefore counterproductive for the government to seek investment abroad while stoking ethnic tensions with ill-advised policies at home. In order to maintain peace and good ethnic relations in the country, policies toward this goal must be intentional. There are several approaches toward attaining this goal but for our purposes and within the limits of this narrative we shall explore social, education, and legislative efforts.

## Social Effort

Because government is felt only in the urban centers and jobs are available in these centers, the tendency has been for migration to occur from the rural peripheries to the urban center. An added push has been insecurity in the rural communities. With a very corrupt and weak police system, armed gangs roam the rural communities and home invasion robberies are common. There are no job opportunities in these communities and the only available job is subsistence farming using very ancient tools. Young men see the move to urban and already populated centers as places to look for work. With anemic electric supply that does not support industrialization, most of these refugees cannot find work. Government policies encourage this outward migration from the rural communities. Rather than build and staff community health centers in rural communities, for example, the government builds expensive teaching hospitals and attaches them to universities in the urban centers for the benefit of the political elites. Rural electrification is nonexistent and access to electric power requires walking miles to buy gasoline for generators that pollute the air. Life is hard, short, and brutish in these conditions and so leaving to the urban centers and a life of an uncertain future becomes attractive.

In the urban environment, the rural migrant learns to trust only those with whom he or she shares a language and culture. He or she joins ethnic and hometown associations in an effort to survive and looks at others as strangers. Social networks are limited and strained and ethnicity thrives. Though no one is proposing the proscription of ethnic associations, rural development as an intentional effort can aid in the development of the country and stem the exodus from rural communities. We shall deal with police reform to deal with the security situation in another section.

## Education

We have already noted, the school system is an arena for sharpened hegemony; this must stop if the government is interested in building good ethnic relations in the country. Nigeria must see diversity as strength and not as a weakness. Laws and policies must encourage the teaching of indigenous languages without the interference of the government. English is already the language of commerce and of communication. Communities who want to codify their tongue as a way of keeping them alive should be allowed to do so. There is no reason to impose a single language on a diverse people when the English language already affords the country the means of communicating with each other. Some intellectual elites have often mentioned that English was imposed on the country by Westerners, yet this same group has done nothing to correct the indirect rule system that is still being practiced today or other colonialists' approaches to solving a problem in a country that they inherited and have benefitted from. It is sheer hypocrisy to be educated in the Western system, learn the language, reap the benefits from some of its provisions, and then move the ladder from others in the name of returning to the indigenous culture.

Education should also try to include multiculturalism and diversity as its goals. Currently, no course is offered in cultural diversity in many of the universities in the country, and so the young waddle in stereotypes and see the other as foreign in their own land.

Additionally, societies where justice and development are the goals tend to value truth over loyalty. In Nigeria, and indeed in Africa, the reverse is the case. Individuals tend to value loyalty over truth and, therefore, are more likely to turn a blind eye over corruption. In this way, unconscious participation in injustice is assured and people work against their own self-interest unknowingly. Individuals may accept corruption and see nothing wrong with it if it is done by a member of their own ethnic group. The attitude tends to be "better my thief than yours." If pushed about the vulgarity of the logic, the response is usually, "What about the individual from the other group who stole?" The Nigerian this way sees a position of influence as a chance for the individual in power to even the scores of embezzlement for the benefit of the team. No one cares whether or not this logic is sound. The liberal arts therefore cannot be neglected in our quest to promote the science, technology, engineering, and mathematics courses. The ability to think critically cannot be overemphasized. In a postmodern world, it is the individual who can think critically who can help solve problems for the self and the nation. The universities and schools have an important part to play in reshaping the Nigeria of the future.

## Politics and Law

Change will be hard to achieve without laws that change old habits and perceptions. As we noted earlier, the tendency has been toward greater separation rather than bringing the country together. As has been demonstrated, the political elites use ethnicity whenever it suits them and the country has continued to lack coherent diversity policy except what the 1999 Constitution refers to as "federal character." Introduced into the polity in 1979 during what is known as the Second Republic, the policy seeks to distribute political and civil service positions according to ethnicity (Falola, 1998). It was seen as a foil against marginalization. Members of ethnic groups see their leaders as speaking for the group when they complain against their group not being represented. There was a widespread belief that an appointment for someone from a particular group is for the benefit of all in the group. With this as a guide, geography became more important than the ability to craft effective policy. Geography triumphs common sense and loyalty is prized above truth. The politicians are very aware of this and so they play the ethnic card at the slightest chance. Political parties currently "zone" positions of power and of governance to different groups. Most Nigerians see this as an issue of justice in a country that practices the politics of plunder. It does not matter that most people who belong to the relevant zone reap very little reward personally. The politicians and their godfathers find the explanation simple to sell to those at home when playing the ethnic card. The ordinary Nigerian feels a sense of being robbed should some politician in his or her linguistic region not be given a coveted position. As noted earlier, it makes very little difference whether the politician in question is personally known to the individual or if the benefits of the position are not communally shared. The average Nigerian has been taught to see communal injury and to forget about sound public policy and the strengthening of institutions of governance. Protected by the dictates of geography from accountability, those whose "turn" it is have little to fear as the nation watches the crumbling of institutions of governance. Because the sense of belonging is very powerful as a secular religion, election day becomes a free for all of violence as individuals see the ballot result as a preservation of their honor; to vote against someone from one's ethnic group means that one is a sellout. Ideas take a back seat and the accident of birth and place of birth become the only reason individuals vote. Groups' sense of entitlement becomes a powerful force that drives violence during elections and beyond. Chaos such as this and loyalty rather than truth are capable of producing strong men and not strong institutions. As President Obama mentioned in his speech to the Ghanaian parliament in 2008, Africa spends much of her time producing strong men and less time fashioning out strong institutions. In the end, institutions are children of ideas and ideas do not die. Unfortunately, men die, and no matter how strong they were, their charisma and toughness die with them. Such "strong men" mentality contribute to the reason Africa produces more dictators than other continents of the world. Thus, planning and policies have tended to lack focus and the issue of ethnicity is not far behind what goes for institutions and state practices.

Nowhere else is this more evident than the present constitution crafted by the Babaginda administration in 1999 in Nigeria. Section 147 (3) of the present constitution requires every state to have a minister in the federal cabinet regardless of need. As I wrote to the Akwa Ibom legislature at the request of a Nigerian group in the United States, the current constitution seems to benefit the center at the expense and detriment of the states. It provides for patronage, and those who are connected to big and powerful men get to benefit from positions assigned to their group. Justice and good governance at the grassroots become difficult and the impact and benefits of government are not felt by the average citizen outside of the urban centers. Of particular concern is the fact that the document is very detailed and has the effect of dictating to the states with very little room for the courts to offer interpretation. Furthermore, though the constitution does not endorse the adoption of a state religion, it prescribes practices of instituting the tenets and faith of one particular religion, namely Islam through the Sharia courts. Another area of concern is the legislative exclusive lists of the central government with more than sixty-eight items designed to stifle growth in an era of rapid information.

The federating units known as states were created by military fiats without any consideration of history, geography, or commerce. The history of federalism in Nigeria is marked by stops and starts and what passes for power sharing between the center and the federating units is lopsided at best and dictatorial at worst. While units in other federations around the world assume a constitutional means of creation, the present Nigerian structures were often created through military decrees. This fact carries an inherent weakness and error. Among these are the neglect of historical ties, the elevation of tribal considerations over economic realities, and the violation of the tenets of social justice. The reality, however, is that the state is the unit through which the oil money is shared and through which political appointments are made. Today the Annang and Ibibio have only one state, while other groups have several states. The irony of this is that the oil wealth in Nigeria is from the south, and those who live close to the oil fields are left to suffer the effects of oil exploration.

The decision to create a state is made arbitrarily and is used as an instrument of domination. Between 1903 and 1945, for example, the British established seventeen provinces in northern Nigeria. Today, those provinces have been turned into twenty states if Ilorin is included as the British did. Old provinces are now called states except in Akwa Ibom where two provinces have been merged into one. The northerners have given themselves more states that allow them to reap a greater share of the oil wealth. Meanwhile, some in the south have seen the demand for more states as fragmentation, while others see it as a threat to homogenization. While some see more state creation for the minority groups as an investment for the future and a means of protection for minority cultures, others see the exercise and agitation as further division and the establishment of cleavages in the country.

## SUGGESTIONS FOR THE FUTURE

The 1999 constitution requires a review with an aim toward unity of the various groups. As Moynihan (1993) noted, the plight and freedom of minority groups need to be taken seriously. The right of self-determination requires that states take responsibility for their own development; therefore, states in the federation should be given the right to craft their own constitution within the bounds of federal law. Currently in Nigeria, states operate without their own constitutions and without their own flags. The governors run their states as fiefdoms, and even the legislature rubber stamps the decision of the governor. The budget is not made public and accountability is poor. As already mentioned, allocation of political office is based on geography and place of origin, therefore the office holder is guaranteed a continued position regardless of performance. A state constitution could curb some of these excesses and ensure practices that are transparent.

One of the most contentious and divisive issue in Nigeria is the role of religion in public life. While the Muslims advocate for the place of religion in public life, the Christian south tends to call for neutrality of the state in religious matters. However, some governors in the Christian south have called for the celebration of major Christian holidays. Akwa Ibom State currently celebrates Christmas and Carol Night during Christmas. Yet nothing compares to the institutionalization of Islam in the country. Though the 1999 constitution prohibits the adoption of a state religion in theory, in practice the judicial system creates two societies: one for Muslims and the other for everyone else. Customary and Sharia courts are prescribed in the constitution that infringe on secular laws made by the national and state assemblies. Having this two-tier system reduces the country to two separate judicial systems and reflects a lack of uniformity. If part II section 1 of the constitution prohibits the adoption of a state religion, one wonders why the state supports a court that is derived from the teachings of a particular religion. In this provision on section 261 (3)(b)1 the pertinent question then becomes: Can a Christian be appointed a Grand Khadi of the Sharia court? The answer is no. Therefore if the constitution implicitly excludes the Christian and non-Muslims from an office and the denial of rights based on religion, such a law is immoral and unjust and is tantamount to the denial of the right of citizenship enumerated in the same constitution. Nigeria consciously or unconsciously is heading toward two societies and two judicial systems, one for the Muslim and the other for the rest of society. If justice is blind, in the Nigerian constitution it is one-eyed, dispensing justice on unequal scale based on faith.

The inclusion of the Customary Court of Appeal as being on par with the Sharia court is an illusion meant to convey the impression that a similar court has been established for non-Muslims. Yet the fact remains that if we are sincere, the reader would realize that the draconian laws of the Sharia, like amputation and stoning, are frowned upon by customary laws of groups in the country. It should be recalled that this holdover from British colonialism was meant to make the implementation of indirect rule imported from India easy for the colonialists as we have already seen. Almost one hundred years after the amalgamation and the introduction of the system, the Nigerian political elites still operate and craft a constitution that echoes the British indirect rule.

Section 275 (1) further entrenches this idea with the provision "There shall be for any State that requires it a Sharia Court of Appeal for that State." The lack of uniformity in the judicial system is further reason why the Sharia court should be removed from the constitution.

Another important issue is the attitude of the political elite class toward security and the control of crime. There seems to be a nonrealization of the knowledge that there is a strong correlation between the adherence to the rule of law and economic prosperity. The unitary police system in a federal democracy does not seem to work. The states and local governments are prohibited from establishing their own police force and all the federating systems depend on poorly trained and poorly equipped federal police. As a result, crime is rampant and the few police officers available are sent to stand guard at the gates of political elites and their well-to-do godfathers. It is not uncommon to find dozens of armed police officers at the gates of politicians' houses while criminal gangs roam the streets terrorizing innocent citizens. The issue of equal justice for all requires that the local government have the power to establish its own police system for the area and be responsible for the security and life of citizens living in that jurisdiction. They should have the power to enforce their own laws including building their own prison subject to the laws and provision of the constitution of the republic. Currently government at the local level cannot establish its own police force and has no power to build prisons, which falls under the exclusive list of the federal government.

Security and law enforcement must be taken seriously. Most ministries in the country have no law enforcement and investigative units and so the police become overwhelmed. There should be an investigative unit for each ministry with the responsibility of investigating violations of relevant ministry rules. Such a unit should be able to monitor police and judicial handling of cases and report to relevant authorities. How such cases are disposed of and an evaluation of such handlings should be mandated by law and such reports should be publicly available. Each state should be made to establish such units in their respective states. Those found to violate the law should be jailed and their ill-gotten wealth confiscated for the benefit of the local law enforcement authority in their jurisdiction. When convicted, what was illegally acquired should be sold and the proceeds used to buy equipment for the local police. The current practice of allowing looters to enjoy their loot in relative comfort is a contributory factor to the current politics of plunder. Additionally, energy should be regarded as a matter of national security. Nigeria cannot modernize, create jobs, and invest in her young people without electricity. It is very difficult to maintain electronic records and track expenditure in the twenty-first century without technology that runs on power, therefore constant power should be seen as a matter of national security. Presidents around the world have made priorities and make certain issues a matter of national security. In the United States, for example, President Eisenhower saw the national highway system as a national security issue and pressed his countrymen to see the issue through such a prism. Today the highway system has brought economic benefits to the United States. The police cannot investigate cases where the system and method of record-keeping are poor.

Evidence abounds that the 1999 constitution was poorly thought out and was designed to benefit the political elites and certain groups at the expense of the development of the country. Unnecessary restrictions are found all over this imperfect document. A few would suffice here: Section 27 (1)(2d) actually puts a restriction on the freedom of the individual with the clause "being acceptable to the local community." Nigerians should be able to live anywhere in Nigeria without going through the hoops of finding out if they are acceptable to the community.

Section 27 (2)(g1) makes immigration cumbersome, difficult, and impossible. Most countries of the world require five years of residency. In Nigeria, fifteen years of residency is required, virtually making it impossible for foreigners to immigrate to the country in this age of globalization. Fifteen years discourages immigration and denies foreigners their service to the country in their youthful days. In a globalized world, rather than discourage immigration, Nigeria should encourage it instead. Studies have shown that societies who accept new ideas grow faster than traditional ones that discourage resettlement of immigrants.

Section 29 (4)(b) defies common sense and is difficult to understand. The section states: "any woman who is married shall be deemed to be of full age." This should be expunged from the constitution of the republic. Though a minimum age of marriage is not given, the section gives sanction to child brides and the abuse of children. There is a potential for international embarrassment should a transnational marriage occur that involves an underage bride. Rather than protects its children, the nation through its constitution provides a vague backdoor for child abuse and child marriage.

The principle of jus soli is absent in the constitution and should be a part of it, allowing a child born in a particular state to claim residency and citizenship of that state regardless of where his or her parents were born in the federation.

Though the country recognizes dual citizenship for Nigerians in the Diaspora, it is not codified in the constitution. Those who live outside of the country in a global age should be given their rights, including the right to vote and be voted for. Individuals should not lose their citizenship and rights because of relocation. A few of the provisions in chapter IV of the constitution are worth mentioning here:

> Section 39 (2) places limits on television and wireless communication in this age of the internet and is capable of stifling growth and innovation.
>
> Section 44 (3) confers all rights to mineral oil, gases, etc. to the federal government. That should be amended and such rights should belong to the community and individuals who own the land, except that prescribed taxes shall be paid to state and the federal government.

In this chapter we have discussed the issues of political plunder and dominance in the current Nigerian state where the Annang live. We also examined the methods of such dominance and identified them as being through education, specifically language policy and the use of fear. We have stressed that harmonious ethnic relation, are more than an academic exercise but have enormous economic implications for international development and investment. In all these, the aim has been to counter the current myth that African economic and political hardships are imposed from the outside. Though one cannot deny the effect of colonialism, the African elites themselves have contributed enormously to the present predicament facing people in the continent. The Africans political elites are not different from the colonialists and in some cases have actually made a bad story worse. We have further made suggestions about ways to improve conditions and move toward sound policies. Perhaps future researchers will examine what future policies fit a continent that has suffered so much.

# References

Achebe, C. (1958). *Things Fall Apart*. Oxford, Heineman Books.
Adams, J. (1823). Remarks on the Country Extending from Cape Palmas to the River Congo. Cited in D. Forde (Eds.), *Efik Traders in Old Calabar*. London: Oxford University Press.
Adeolu, A. (2017). *Olusegun Obasanjo: Nigeria's Most Successful Ruler*. Ibadan, Nigeria: Safari Books Ltd.
Ake, C. (1992). What Is the Problem of Ethnicity in Africa? Keynote address at the Conference on Ethnicity, Society, and Conflict, University of Natal, South Africa.
Akhtar, S. (1999). *Immigration and Identity: Turmoil, Treatment, and Transformation*. Northvale, NJ: Jason Aronson, Inc.
Akpan, N. U. (1967). *Epitaph to Indirect Rule: A Discourse on Local Government in Africa*. London: Frank Cass and Co. Ltd.
*Akwa Ibom State Government News Online*. Mboho Mkparawa Breaks Ethnic Barrier. http://www.akwaibomnewsonline.com/news/index.php?url=http://aksgonline.com/articlePage.aspx?qrID=594.
Albright, D. (2004). *Modernism and Music: An Anthology of Sources*. Chicago: University of Chicago Press.
Aluko, S. A. (1969). The Problem of the Displaced Persons in Falope. J. A. I. and E. Urhobo (Eds.), *Christian Concern in the Nigerian Civil War*. Ibadan, Nigeria: Daystar Press.
Anene, J. C. (1966). *Southern Nigeria in Transition, 1885–1906: Theory and Practice in Colonial Protectorate*. London: Cambridge University Press.
Atkinson, P., and Hammersley, M. (1994). Ethnography and Participant Observation. In N. K. Denzin and S. Y. Lincoln (Eds.), *Handbook of Qualitative Research*. Thousand Oaks, CA: Sage Publications.
Ayandele, E. A. (1966). *The Missionary Impact on Modern Nigeria 1842–1914*. London: Oxford University Press.
Aye, E. U. (1987). *Presbyterianism in Nigeria*. Calabar, Nigeria: Wusen Press.

Barrett, D. B. (1968). Schism and Renewal in Africa, Lusaka. Quoted in J. B. Ekanem. (2002). *Clashing Cultures: Annang Not(with)standing Christianity—An Ethnography.* Bruxelles, P.I.E.: Peter Lang.

Beatie, J. (1953). Review of *The Missionary Factor in East Africa* by R. Oliver. *Journal of the Royal Anthropological Institute,* 83, 178.

Becker, H. C., Geer, B., Hughes, E. C., and Strauss, A. L. (1961). *Boys in White.* Chicago: University of Chicago Press.

Bell, D. (Ed.) (2014). *Masquerade: Essays on Tradition and Innovation Worldwide.* Jefferson, NC: McFarland and Co. Pub.

Bennett, M. J. (2017). Developmental Model of Intercultural Sensitivity. In *The International Encyclopedia of Intercultural Communication.* Boston, MA: John Wiley and Sons, Inc.

Betancourt, H., and López, S. R. (1993). The Study of Culture, Ethnicity, and Race in American Psychology. *American Psychologist,* 48(6), 629–37.

Boer, J. H. (1988). *Christianity and Islam Under Colonialism in Northern Nigeria.* Jos, Nigeria: Institute of Church and Society.

Bourdeau, M. (2015). Auguste Comte. *The Stanford Encyclopedia of Philosophy* (Winter 2015 Edition), Edward N. Zalta (Ed.). https://plato.stanford.edu/archives/win2015/entries/comte/.

Briggs, H., and Paulson, R. (1996). Racism in Finding Solutions to Social Problems. In M. A. Mattan and B. A. Thyers (Eds.), *Behavioral Strategies for Change.* Washington, DC: APA.

Brink, P. J. (1982). Traditional Birth Attendants among the Annang of Nigeria: Current Practices and Proposed Programs. *Social Science and Medicine,* 16(21), 1883–92.

Chambers, D. B. (2005). *Murder at Montpelier: Igbo Africans in Virginia.* Jackson: University Press of Mississippi.

Clark, T. J. (1999). *Farewell to an Idea: Episodes from a History of Modernism.* New Haven, CT: Yale University Press.

Comte, A. (1853). *The Positive Philosophy of Auguste Comte, Vol. II* (in 2 volumes). New York: Cosimo Classics.

Connell, B. (1994). The Lower Cross Languages: A Prolegomena to the Classification of Cross River Languages. *Journal of West African Languages,* 24(1).

Davis, J. M. (1933). *Modern Industry and the African.* London: Macmillan and Co.

Decker, C. R. (1952). *The Victorian Conscience.* New York: Twayne Publishers

Denzin. N. K. (1989). *Interpretive Interactionism.* Newbury Park: Sage Publications.

Denzin, N., and Lincoln, Y. S. (1994). Entering the Field of Qualitative Research. In N. Denzin and Y. S. Lincoln (Eds.), *Handbook of Qualitative Research.* Thousand Oaks, CA: Sage Publications.

Duke, Antera. (1785). The Diary of Antera Duke. In D. Forde (Ed.), *Efik Traders in Old Calabar.* London: Oxford University Press.

Durkheim, E. (1912). *Elementary Forms of the Religious Life.* Mineola, NY: Dover Publications Inc.

*The Economist.* (2016). Bloodshed in Central Africa: Burundian Time-Bomb. 419(8986).

Ekanem, J. B. (2002). *Clashing Cultures: Annang Not(with)standing Christianity— An Ethnography.* Bruxelles, P.I.E.: Peter Lang.

Ekeh, P. P., and Osaghae, E. E. (Eds.) (1989). *Federal Character and Federalism in Nigeria.* Ibadan, Nigeria: Heinemann Educational Books.

Enang, K. (1982). *The African Experience of Salvation: Based on the Annang Independent Churches of Nigeria.* London: M and C Publishing.

Enang, K. (1987). Some key religious concepts of the annang. Cross River Religion / Edited by Rosalind I.j. Hackett, Pages 21–35.

Engels, F. (1978). The Origin of the Family, Private Property and the State. In R. C. Tucker (Ed.), *The Marx-Engels Reader.* New York: W. W. Norton and Co.

Erikson, E. H (1958) Young Man Luther: A Study in Psychoanalysis and History.

Ette, E. (2012). *Nigerian Immigrants in the United States: Race Identity and Acculturation.* Lanham, MD: Lexington Books.

Ette, E. (2010). The Scientific Enterprise, Identity and Power in Africa: The Case of the Annang of Nigeria. *The International Journal of Science in Society,* 4(1), 215–25.

Ette, E. (2009). *Annang Wisdom: Tools for Post Modern Living.* Bloomington, IN: Xlibir Press.

Ette, E. (2001). Social Reform, Missionary Efforts and the Contribution of Women in Southeast Nigeria 1846–1914. Paper presented at the Women in the Making of the Black World International Conference, the University of Houston, Houston, Texas.

Etounga-Manguelle, D. (2000). Does Africa Need a Cultural Adjustment Program? In L. E. Harrison and S. P. Huntington (Eds.), *Culture Matters: How Values Shape Human Progress.* New York: Basic Books.

Ewelukwa, U. U. (2005). Centuries of Globalization; Centuries of Exclusion: African Women, Human Rights and the "New" International Trade Regime. *Berkley Journal of Gender, Law and Justice,* 20, 75–149.

Fafunwa, A. B. (1974). *History of Education in Nigeria.* London: George Allen and Unwin.

Falola, T. (1998). *Violence in Nigeria: The Crisis of Religious Politics and Secular Ideologies.* Rochester, NY: University of Rochester Press.

Farb, P. (1974). *Word Play: What Happens When People Talk.* New York: Alfred Knopf Publishers.

Forde, D. (Ed.) (1956). *Efik Traders of Old Calabar.* London: Oxford University Press.

Forde, D., and Jones, G. I. (1950). *The Ibo and Ibibio Speaking Peoples of South Eastern Nigeria.* London: Oxford University.

Forsyth, F. (1969) *The Biafran Story: The Making of the African Legend.* Barnsley, England. Pen and Sword Military.

Freire, P. (1970). *Pedagogy of the Oppressed.* New York: Bloomsbury Publishing Inc.

Gardner, G. B. (1959). *The Meaning of Witchcraft.* New York: Samuel Weiser Inc.

Gladwin, H. C. (1989). *Ethnographic Decision Tree.* Newbury Park: Sage Publications.

Gore, C. (1995) *Social Exclusion: Rhetoric, Reality, Responses* (co-edited with G. Rodgers and J.B. Figueiredo). International Institute for Labour Studies, Geneva.

Gore, C., and Pratten, D. (2003). The Politics of Plunder: The Rhetorics of Order and Disorder in Southern Nigeria. *African Affairs,* 102, 211–40.

Greenwood, D. J. (1985). Castilians, Basques, and Andalusians: An Historical Comparison of Nationalism, "True" Ethnicity and "False" Ethnicity. In P. Brass (Ed.), *Ethnic Groups and the State*. Totowa, NJ: Barnes and Noble.

Groves, C. P. (1948). *The Planting of Christianity in Africa, Vol. 1*. London: Lutterworth Press. Cited in T. Falola. (1998). *Violence in Nigeria: The Crisis of Religious Politics and Secular Ideologies*. Rochester, NY: University of Rochester Press.

Groves, W. (1936). The Story of Udo Akpabio of the Anang Tribe, Southern Nigeria. In M. Perham (Ed.), *Ten Africans*. London: Faber and Faber Ltd.

Hardage, J. (2002). The Legacy of Mary Slessor. *International Bulletin of Missionary Research, 4*, 178–81.

Harris, M. (2001). *The Rise of Anthropological Theory: A History of Theories of Culture*. Lanham, MD: Altamira Press.

Healy, L. M. (2001). *International Social Work: Professional Action in an Interdependent World*. New York: Oxford University Press Books.

Horwitz, P. (2007). Uncovering Identity. *Michigan Law Review, 105*(6), 1283–1300.

Hughes, D., Rodriguez, J., Smith, E. P., Johnson, D. J., Stevenson, H. C., and Spicer, P. (2006). *Parents' Ethnic–Racial Socialization Practices: A Review of Research and Directions for Future Study*. Developmental Psychology, 42(5), 747–70.

Igwara, O. (2001). Dominance and Difference: Rival Visions of Ethnicity in Nigeria. *Ethnic and Racial Studies, 24*(1), 86–103.

Imbua, D. L (2013) Old Calabar Merchants and the Offshore British Community 1650–1750. *Paideuma*: Mitteilungen zur Kulturkunde Bd. 59, 51–75.

Jones, G. I. (1989). Recollections of the Spirit Movement in the Ibibio Area of Calabar Province. *Africa, 4*(59), 555–58.

Isaacs, H. (1975). *Idols of the Tribe: Group Identity and Political Change*. New York: Harper and Row. Quoted in D. P. Moynihan. (1993). *Pandaemonium: Ethnicity in International Politics*. New York: Oxford University Press.

Jones, H. S. (Ed.) (1998). *Augustus Comte: Early Political Writings*. Cambridge: Cambridge University Press.

Kenyatta, J. (1938). *Facing Mount Kenya*. London: Secker and Warburge.

Kidder, D. S., and Oppenheim, N. D. (2005). *The Intellectual Devotional*. New York: Rodale Inc.

Kilty, K. M., and Haymes, M. V. D. (2004). What's in A Name? Racial and Ethnic Classifications and the Meaning of Hispanic/Latino in the United States. *Ethnic Studies Review, 27*(1), 32–56.

King, M. L. K (1963) Letter From Birmingham Jail In *I have A Dream: Letters and Speeches that Changed the World*. Washington, J. M (ed) San Francisco, Harper.

Kolapo, F. M. (2004). The Igbo and Rheir Neighbors during the Era of the Atlantic Slave-Trade. *Slavery and Abolition, 25*(1), 114–33.

Kroeber, T. (1961). *Ishi in Two Worlds*. Berkeley: University of California Press.

Law, A. (2015). *Social Theory for Today: Making Sense of Social Worlds*. Thousand Oaks, CA: Sage Publications.

Latham, A. J. H. (1973). *Old Calabar 1600–1891: The Impact of the International Economy Upon a Traditional Society*. Oxford: Clarendon Press.

Letter from the Governor, Nigeria. Quoted in J. A. G. McCall. (1986). Comment on the Leopard Killings. *Africa, 56*(4), 441–45.

Letters to Mr. Partridge. http://www.dundeecity.gov.uk/centlib/slessor/letext0.htm.

Lewis, P. (2011). *The Cambridge Companion to European Modernism*. New York: Cambridge University Press.

Livingstone, W. P. (1916). *Mary Slessor of Calabar: Pioneer Missionary*. London: Hodder and Stoughton.

Losch, B., Fregun-Gresh, S., and White, E. T. (Eds.) (2012). *Structural Transformation and Rural Change Revisited: Challenges for Late Developing Countries in a Globalizing World*. Washington, DC: The World Bank.

Lukacs, John. (2003). *At the End of an Age*. New Haven, CT: Yale University Press.

Lyotard, Jean-Francois (1979). *Introduction: The Postmodern Condition: A Report on Knowledge*, xxiv–xxv. http://www.idehist.uu.se/distans/ilmh/pm/lyotard-introd.htm.

Marcus, G. E. (1994). What Comes (Just) After "Post"?: The Case of Ethnography. In N. Denzin and Y. S. Lincoln (Eds.), *Handbook of Qualitative Research*. Thousand Oaks, CA: Sage Publications.

Martineau, H. (Trans.) (2009). A. Comte. (1853). *The Positive Philosophy of Auguste Comte, Vol. II* (in 2 volumes). New York: Cosimo Classics.

Marwick, W. (1897). *William and Louisa Anderson: A Record of Their Life and Work in Jamaica and Old Calabar*. Edinburgh: Andrew Elliott.

Mbembe, A. (2001). *On the Postcolony*. Berkeley, CA: University of California Press.

Meek, C. K. (1937) *Law and Authority in a Nigerian Tribe*. Oxford: Oxford University Press.

Mehta, V. (1997). Ethnic Conflict and Violence in the Modern World: Social Work's Role in Building Peace. In M. C. Hokenstad and J. Midgley (Eds.), *Issues in International Social Work*. Washington, DC: NASW Press.

Messenger, J. C. (1957). Anang Acculturation: A Study of Shifting Cultural Focus. Unpublished doctoral dissertation, Northwestern University, Evanston, IL.

Minutes of the Ibibio Welfare Union. (1928). In E. N. Noah (Ed.), *Proceedings of the Ibibio Union 1928–1937*. Uyo, Nigeria: Modern Business Press.

Moynihan, D. P. (1993). *Pandaemonium: Ethnicity in International Politics*. New York: Oxford University Press.

Murdock, G. P. (1934). *Our Primitive Contemporaries*. New York: The Macmillan Co.

Nair, Kaanan K. (1972). *Politics and Society in South Eastern Nigeria, 1841–1906*. London: Frank Cass.

Neuman, W. L. (1997). *Social Research Methods*. Boston: Allyn and Bacon.

Newton, John. (1750). Thoughts Upon the African Slave Trade. In B. Martin and M. Spurell (Eds.) (1962), *The Journal of a Slave Trader*. London: Epworth Press.

Noah, M. E. (1988). *Proceedings of the Ibibio Union 1928–1937*. Uyo, Nigeria: Modern Business Press.

Noah, M. E. (1987a). After the Warrant Chiefs: Native Authority Rule in Ibibioland 1931–1951. *Phylon, 48*(1), 77–90.

Noah, M. E. (1987b). The Ibibio Union 1928–1966. *Canadian Journal of African Studies, 21*(1), 38–53.

Nwaka, G. I. (1986). The Leopards' Killings of Southern Annang, Nigeria, 1943–48. *Africa,* 56(4), 417–40.

Obianyo, N. E. (2008). Behind the Curtains of State Power: Religious Groups and the Struggle for Ascendancy in Nigerian Public Institutions: A Critical Appraisal Codestria, 12th General Assembly, Yaounde, Cameroun.

Obioha, E. E. A. (1999). Ethnic Conflicts and the Problem of Resolution in Contemporary Africa: A Case for African Options and Alternatives. In *Anthropology of Africa and the Challenges of the Third Millennium—Ethnicity and Ethnic Conflicts.* Enugu, Nigeria: PAAA/APA.

O'Connell, J. (1969). The Politics of Instability in Falope, J. A. and Urhobo, I. E. (Ed.), *Christian Concern in the Nigerian Civil War.* Ibadan, Nigeria: Daystar Press.

Offiong, D. A. (1991). *Witchcraft, Sorcery, Magic and Social Order Among the Ibibio of Nigeria.* Enugu, Nigeria: Fourth Dimension Publishing Co.

Pratten, D. (2006) The Politics of Vigilance in Southeastern Nigeria. *Development and Change.* 37(4) 707–34.

Pratten, D. (2007) *The Man-Leopard Murders: History and Society in Colonial Nigeria.* Bloomington, Indiana, Indiana University Press.

Perham, M. (1936). *Ten Africans.* London: Faber and Faber Ltd.

*Pioneer Newsonline.* (2018). Info Boss Makes Case for Revival of Mother Language. http://www.pioneernewsonline.com/news/info-boss-makes-case-for-revival-of-mother-language.

Primitive Methodist Missionary Society: Archive Record (2007). http://www.genesis.ac.uk/archive.jsp?typeofsearch=q&term=notimpl&highlight=1&pk=30.

Reese, W. L. (1980). *Dictionary of Philosophy and Religion: Eastern and Western Thought.* Atlantic Highlands, NJ: Humanities Press Inc.

Report of the Commission of Inquiry Appointed to Inquire into the Disturbances in the Calabar and Owerri Provinces. (1929). Aba Commission of Inquiry. Reprinted in The Igbo "Women's War" of 1929; Documents Relating to the Aba Riots in Eastern Nigeria. D.C. Doward (Ed.) (1983), Microform Limited.

Report of the Tour of Ibibio Delegates in the Man-Leopard Areas of Abak—Opobo and Uyo Division of the Calabar Province, July 26 to 31, 1947, OP287/C, Opdist, NAE.

Rodney, W. (1974). *How Europe Under Developed Africa.* Washington, DC: Howard Press.

Roe, E. (1999). *Except-Africa: Remaking Development, Rethinking Power*, New Brunswick, NJ: Transactions.

Schwandt, T. A. (1994). Constructivist, Interpretivist Approaches to Human Inquiry. In N. Denzin and Y. S. Lincoln (Eds.), *Handbook of Qualitative Research.* Thousand Oaks, CA: Sage Publications.

Seagal, M., and Doornbos, M. (1976). Becoming Ugandan: The Dynamics of Identity in a Multicultural African State. Syracuse University Foreign and Comparative Series 24.

Service, E. R. (1958). *A Profile of Primitive Culture.* New York: Harper and Brothers Publishers.

Simmons, D. (1956). An Ethnographic Sketch of the Efik People. In D. Forde (Ed.), *The Efik Traders of Old Calabar*. Oxford: Oxford University Press.

Stevenson, H. C., Herrero-Taylor, T., Cameron, R., and Davis, G. Y. (2002). "Mitigating Instigation": Cultural Phenomenological Influences of Anger and Fighting among "Big-Boned" and "Baby-Faced" African American Youth. *Journal of Youth and Adolescence, 31*, 473–85.

Talbot, P. A. (1926). The People of Southern Nigeria. Cited in D. Forde (Ed.), *The Efik Traders of Old Calabar*. Oxford: Oxford University Press.

Talbot, P. A. (1923). *Life in Southern Nigeria*. London: Macmillan Ltd.

Talbot, D. A. (1915). *Woman's Mysteries of a Primitive People*. London: Cassell and Co. Ltd.

This Day. (2002). Potiskum's Challenge to Damaturu as Yobe Capital. August 26. http://allafrica.com/stories/200208260432.html.

Travis, H. (2013) *Genocide, Ethnonationalism and the United Nations: Exploring the causes of Mass Killings Since 1945*. New York, New York, Routledge.

Udo, E. U. (1983). *The History of the Annang People*. Calabar, Nigeria: Apcon Press Ltd.

Udoma U. (1988). Foreword to the Proceedings of the Ibibio Union 1928–1937. In M. E. Noah, (Ed.), *Proceedings of the Ibibio Union 1928–1937*. Uyo, Nigeria: Modern Business Press.

Uzoigwe, G. N. (2004). Evolution and Relevance of Autonomous Communities in Precolonial Igboland. *Journal of Third World Studies, 21*(1), 139–50.

Vidich, A. J., and Lyman, S. M. (1994). Qualitative Methods: Their History in Sociology and Anthropology. In N. Denzin and Y. S. Lincoln (Eds.), *Handbook of Qualitative Research*. Thousand Oaks, CA: Sage Publications

Waddell, H. M. (1863). *Thirty-Nine Years in the West Indies and Central Africa: A Review of Missionary Work and Adventure 1829–1858*. London: Frank Cass Ltd.

Waugh, A. (1894). Reticence in Literature, Yellow Book I. Quoted in C. R. Decker. (1952). *The Victorian Conscience*. New York: Twayne Publishers.

Weisner, T. S. (2000). Culture, Childhood, and Progress in Sub-Saharan Africa. In L. E. Harrison and S. P. Huntington (Eds.), *Culture Matters: How Values Shape Human Progress*. New York: Basic Books.

Young, C. (1985). Ethnicity and the Colonial and Post Colonial State in Africa. In P. Brass (Ed.), *Ethnic Groups and the State*. Totowa, NJ: Barnes and Noble.

Zastrow, C. (1989). *Social Work with Groups*. Chicago: Nelson-Hall.

# Index

Abak, 48, 91
Afaha, 12
African Club, 98
Aggrey, 87
agricultural guilds, 25–26, 27
alien, 2
Akan, 12
Ankole Pattern, 50
arrested development, 117
Aros, 40–41, 45

boundaries, 4

Christian duty, 44
Civil Right Movement, 8
Comtean, 5

Democratic Republic of Congo, 50

education, 89–90
    women, 92
Egbo Sharry, 31, 41
Egypt, 12
Eket, 91
Emic perspective, 115
ethnic, 2
    conflict, 2
ethnicity, 14–15

ethnography, 114–16
Etic perspective, 115
Etinan, 91
evangelization, 38

Fattening Ceremony, 18
Fernado Po, 35, 37, 38, 87

globalization, 2, 3,
Ghana, 12

hegemony, 44, 88, 106
homogenization, 119
House of Commons, 34

Ibrahim Babangida, 136
Ifuho, 46–47
Ikot Abasi, 48
Ikot Ekpene, 43, 46, 48, 91, 98
Ikot Ekpene Society, 92
Ikot Ekpene Hope Rising Club, 101
Ikot Udobong Wars, 11
impermanence, 6
India, 50
intellectualism, 44
International Country Risk Guide, 139

Jamaica, 35

King Jaja of Opobo, 11–12
Kwashiokor, 131

leopard killings, 48, 96, 104
Long Juju, 40

machete, 43
magistrate court, 101
Mami Wata, 29
manifest and latent goals, 103
melting pot, 5
messenger, 11
Ministry of Local Government and Chieftaincy Affairs, 136

native court, 101
Native Teaching Evangelists Model, 87
New Yam Festival, 26
noble savage, 117
Ntinya, 23
Nyama, 22

palm oil, 15,
palm kernel, 15
Paramount Ruler, 136
politics of plunder, 142, 146
polygamy, 24
positivism, 5–6

realism, 44
The Richards Constitution, 93

superior court, 101
Sahara Desert, 12
slave trade, 15, 33, 36–37
same-sex marriage, 23
Southern Nigeria Mission, 87

taboo, 12
    food, 12–13, 18
    twins, 15
Talbot, 11, 122, 123
theories
    ethnocentric, 6
    evolutionary, 6
Tuskegee Institute, 90

Udo Umo Ekam, 17
Uganda, 50
Ukanafun, 48, 109
Ukpong Inokon, 46
Uyo, 48

village square, 25

warrior society, 18, 22, 43, 62
witchcraft, 29

# About the Author

**Dr. Ette** received his bachelor's degree in secondary education from the University of Tennessee and his theological education from Emory University in Atlanta, Georgia, where he earned the MDiv degree. He studied gerontology at Georgia State University and later obtained MSW and PhD degrees from Portland State University in Portland, Oregon. He joined the faculty of social work at Indiana University following his doctoral studies before going back west to teach and direct research. After almost ten years of work in the western United States, Dr. Ette returned to the East Coast to head the only social work program in the State of Delaware at Delaware State University. His specialties are in the areas of immigration, refugees, culture, health policy, spirituality, and social history. He has presented papers at national and international conferences and is the author of several books and monographs. His passion for the preservation of African indigenous languages led to the formation of the Preservation of Threatened African Languages (POTAL). The organization seeks to codify nonarchival languages and to teach such languages to the next generation in order to preserve them. This effort has already yielded fruit with the invention of orthography and the publication of books for the first four years of primary school in one language. Dr. Ette and his wife, Nse, are the proud parents of two young men.

www.ingramcontent.com/pod-product-compliance
Lightning Source LLC
Chambersburg PA
CBHW020124010526
44115CB00008B/964